Diabetic Diet Cookbook for Beginners

Discover Over 2000 Days of Super Easy, Delicious Low-Carb, Low-Sugar Recipes for Managing Prediabetes & Type 2 | A 30-Day Meal Plan for Building Healthy Habits After 50

Feast on Healthy Recipes with Exquisite Flavor

Daniel Pierce

TABLE OF CONTENTS

INTRODUCTION

Welcome to the Diabetic Diet Cookbook, a comprehensive guide for those looking to take control of their health through a balanced and flavorful approach to eating. As a professional chef with years of experience in creating nutritious and delicious meals, I'm excited to share with you the principles and benefits of a diabetic-friendly diet, along with a carefully curated selection of recipes that will delight your taste buds while supporting your health goals.

This cookbook is more than just a collection of recipes; it's a tool to help you manage your diabetes with confidence and creativity in the kitchen.

Meal Plans

You'll find a 30-day meal plan that takes the guesswork out of planning your meals, ensuring you have a balanced and enjoyable diet every day. Each week is thoughtfully organized to provide variety while keeping your blood sugar levels stable.

Recipes

The recipes are divided into categories, including breakfasts, lunches, dinners, snacks, and desserts, making it easy to find what you need. Each recipe has been carefully crafted to meet the dietary needs of people with diabetes, focusing on low glycemic index ingredients, balanced nutrients, and ease of preparation.

Nutritional Information

Each recipe includes nutritional facts and glycemic index information to help you make informed choices. This will allow you to manage your carbohydrate intake and keep your blood sugar levels in check.

Shopping Guide

To make following the 30-Day Meal Plan even more convenient, a detailed Shopping Guide is provided, breaking down the essential ingredients you'll need for each week. This guide simplifies your grocery shopping, ensuring you have everything you need to prepare the meals in the plan.

By following these guidelines and enjoying the meals in this book, you can take charge of your health and well-being. Set out on this culinary journey and experience the benefits of a balanced, diabetes-friendly diet. Let's get cooking!

Yours in culinary health,
Daniel Pierce.

CHAPTER 1: Diabetic Diet Basics

Understanding Diabetes

Diabetes is a chronic condition that affects how your body processes blood sugar (glucose). There are two main types of diabetes:

Type 1	Type 2
Diabetes is an autoimmune condition where the body attacks insulin-producing cells in the pancreas, leading to little or no insulin production. People with Type 1 diabetes must manage their blood sugar levels through insulin therapy, diet, and lifestyle adjustments.	Diabetes is more common and is often related to lifestyle factors. In Type 2 diabetes, the body becomes resistant to insulin or doesn't produce enough of it, leading to high blood sugar levels. It can often be managed through diet, exercise, and medication.

Both types of diabetes require careful monitoring and management of blood sugar levels, and diet plays a crucial role in this process.

The Role of Diet in Managing Diabetes

Diet plays a crucial role in the effective management of diabetes. What you eat directly impacts your blood sugar levels, making it essential to choose foods that help maintain stable glucose levels, support weight management, and reduce the risk of complications such as heart disease.

A well-balanced diabetic diet focuses on several key nutritional principles:

Low Glycemic Index (GI) Foods

These foods cause a slower, more gradual rise in blood sugar levels, helping to prevent spikes. Examples include whole grains, non-starchy vegetables, and certain fruits.

Controlled Carbohydrate Intake

Monitoring the type and amount of carbohydrates consumed is critical for blood sugar control. Each recipe in this cookbook is designed with carbohydrate limits suitable for diabetes management.

Fiber-Rich Foods

High-fiber foods are essential as they slow down sugar absorption, helping to regulate blood sugar levels. Including plenty of vegetables, legumes, and whole grains in your diet can enhance fiber intake.

Healthy Fats and Proteins

Incorporating healthy fats from sources like nuts, seeds, and fish, along with lean proteins, helps keep you full, supports heart health, and maintains overall well-being.

Limiting Added Sugars

This cookbook emphasizes reducing added sugars, using natural or sugar-free sweeteners as needed, ensuring that your meals are both satisfying and supportive of blood sugar management.

Portion Control

Proper portion sizes are vital for maintaining blood sugar levels within a healthy range. The serving sizes in this cookbook are carefully measured to provide balanced, diabetes-friendly portions.

What to Eat and What to Avoid

Managing diabetes involves making informed choices about what to eat and what to avoid. The right foods can help you maintain stable blood sugar levels, manage your weight, and reduce the risk of complications.

What to Eat	What to Avoid
Low Glycemic Index (GI) Foods Focus on whole grains, non-starchy vegetables, legumes, and certain fruits like berries and apples.	**High Glycemic Index (GI) Foods** Avoid refined grains, sugary drinks, and processed foods that cause rapid spikes in blood sugar.
Lean Proteins Include sources like chicken, turkey, fish, eggs, and tofu, which help keep you full and support muscle health.	**Added Sugars** Minimize consumption of sugary snacks, desserts, and beverages, opting for natural or sugar-free alternatives.
Healthy Fats Incorporate unsaturated fats from sources like avocados, nuts, seeds, and olive oil to support heart health.	**Saturated and Trans Fats** Limit foods high in unhealthy fats like fried foods, processed meats, and full-fat dairy products.
Fiber-Rich Foods Vegetables, whole grains, and legumes help regulate blood sugar and improve digestion.	**Excessive Salt** Reduce intake of salty foods, which can contribute to high blood pressure, a common concern for people with diabetes.

Understanding Carbohydrates and Sugar

Carbohydrates are a key factor in diabetes management because they have a direct impact on blood sugar levels. Understanding the types of carbohydrates and their effects on your body is crucial for maintaining stable glucose levels.

Simple Carbohydrates:
Found in foods like sugary snacks, white bread, and sweetened beverages, these carbs are quickly absorbed and can cause rapid blood sugar spikes. They should be limited or avoided.

Complex Carbohydrates:
Found in whole grains, vegetables, and legumes, these carbs are digested more slowly, leading to a more gradual rise in blood sugar. These should be the main source of carbohydrates in your diet.

Sugar:
Natural sugars, like those found in fruits, are generally better choices than added sugars. However, portion control is important, even with natural sugars, to avoid spikes in blood sugar.

The Role of Glycemic Index (GI) in Diabetes Management

The Glycemic Index (GI) is a tool that ranks foods based on how quickly they raise blood sugar levels. Understanding and using the GI can help you make better food choices to manage your diabetes.

Low GI Foods
(GI score 55 or less)

These foods cause a slower and more stable rise in blood sugar. Examples include non-starchy vegetables, whole grains, and most fruits.

Medium GI Foods
(GI score 56-69)

These foods have a moderate impact on blood sugar. Examples include whole wheat products and certain fruits like bananas.

High GI Foods
(GI score 70 or higher)

These foods cause rapid spikes in blood sugar and should be limited. Examples include white bread, sugary cereals, and snacks.

Incorporating more low GI foods into your diet can help maintain steady blood sugar levels, reduce the risk of complications, and improve overall health.

Cholesterol and Diabetes: What You Need to Know

Diabetes can significantly impact your cholesterol levels, which in turn affects your heart health. Understanding the relationship between diabetes and cholesterol is vital for managing both conditions effectively.

LDL ("Bad") Cholesterol

High levels of LDL cholesterol can lead to plaque buildup in arteries, increasing the risk of heart disease. People with diabetes are often more prone to having high LDL levels.

HDL ("Good") Cholesterol

HDL cholesterol helps remove LDL cholesterol from the bloodstream, protecting heart health. Increasing your HDL levels can be beneficial, especially for those with diabetes.

Triglycerides

These are another type of fat in the blood, and high levels can also increase the risk of heart disease, particularly in people with diabetes.

To manage cholesterol levels, focus on reducing saturated fats and trans fats, incorporating more healthy fats, and eating fiber-rich foods. Regular exercise and weight management are also key components of maintaining healthy cholesterol levels.

Portion Control and Meal Planning Tips

Portion control is critical for managing diabetes, as eating too much — even of healthy foods — can lead to spikes in blood sugar. Here are some tips to help you manage portions and plan meals effectively:

Portion Control	Meal Planning
Use Smaller Plates This simple trick can help control portion sizes and prevent overeating.	**Plan Ahead** Create a weekly meal plan that includes balanced meals and snacks. This can help you avoid last-minute unhealthy choices.
Balance Your Plate Aim to fill half your plate with non-starchy vegetables, a quarter with lean protein, and a quarter with whole grains or starchy vegetables.	**Batch Cooking** Prepare large portions of healthy meals that you can freeze or refrigerate for later in the week. This makes it easier to stick to your diet.
Measure Portions Use measuring cups or a food scale to ensure you're eating the right amount of each food group.	**Mind Your Snacks** Choose snacks that are low in carbs and high in fiber or protein, like nuts, seeds, or low-fat yogurt.

Dining-Out and at Social Events

Eating out or attending social events can be challenging when managing diabetes, but with some preparation and mindfulness, you can make healthy choices:

Before You Go

- **Plan Ahead:** If possible, check the restaurant's menu online before you go. Look for dishes that fit your dietary needs, such as grilled meats, salads, or dishes with vegetables.

- **Eat a Snack:** Have a small, healthy snack before heading out to avoid overeating or choosing unhealthy options.

At the Restaurant or Event

- **Choose Wisely:** Opt for grilled, baked, or steamed dishes rather than fried or sautéed. Ask for dressings and sauces on the side.

- **Control Portions:** Restaurant portions are often larger than necessary. Consider sharing a meal with someone or asking for a to-go box right away and saving half for later.

- **Limit Alcohol:** Alcohol can affect blood sugar levels. If you choose to drink, do so in moderation and avoid sugary mixers.

In Social Situations

- **Bring a Dish:** If attending a potluck or gathering, offer to bring a dish that you know is diabetes-friendly. This ensures there will be something healthy for you to eat.

- **Stay Hydrated:** Drink plenty of water, and avoid sugary drinks or excessive alcohol.

- **Mindful Eating:** Enjoy the food, but be mindful of your portion sizes and avoid going back for seconds if you're already satisfied.

With these strategies, you can enjoy dining out and social events while still keeping your diabetes management on track.

Conclusion

Managing diabetes through diet requires knowledge, planning, and mindful choices, but it doesn't have to mean sacrificing flavor or enjoyment. By understanding the basics outlined in this chapter, you're equipped to make informed decisions that support your health. With the right approach, you can enjoy a wide variety of delicious meals while effectively managing your blood sugar levels.

CHAPTER 2: Quick and Easy Kitchen Hacks for Effortless Cooking

Cooking Hacks

Use a slow cooker or pressure cooker

These appliances will save you time and ensure your dishes retain more nutrients. Perfect for busy weeknights when you still want a homemade meal.

Steam your veggies

Steaming is one of the healthiest ways to cook vegetables, preserving their vitamins and minerals without needing added fats.

Batch cook and freeze portions

Make larger quantities of soups, stews, or grains and freeze them in individual portions. This makes it easy to grab a healthy meal when you're short on time.

Use silicone baking molds

These non-stick molds don't need oil, keeping your dishes lighter and reducing unnecessary fats.

Ingredient Prep & Cutting Hacks

Quick garlic peeling

Place garlic cloves in a bowl, cover it with a plate, and shake vigorously for a few seconds. The skins will slip right off.

Tomato peeling made easy

Blanch tomatoes by dunking them in boiling water for 30 seconds, then immediately into ice water. The skins will peel away easily.

Chop herbs quickly with scissors

Skip the chopping board and use kitchen scissors to snip herbs directly into your dishes for fast, mess-free prep.

Keep knives sharp

A sharp knife makes prep faster and safer. It requires less pressure, reducing the chance of accidents.

Grain Cooking Hacks

Soak grains overnight

Soaking grains like quinoa, barley, or farro cuts down cooking time and makes them easier to digest. This also helps unlock more of their nutrients.

Perfect water-to-grain ratios

For quinoa, use a 1:2 ratio (1 cup quinoa to 2 cups water); for rice, 1:2.5. These ratios ensure grains cook to the right texture every time.

Add spices while cooking grains

Toss in a bay leaf, some garlic, or a pinch of turmeric while grains are simmering. It infuses them with flavor, turning a simple side dish into something special.

Cook grains in broth instead of water

Using vegetable or chicken broth gives grains a rich, savory flavor without the need for extra salt or butter.

Weight Control Hacks

Drink water before meals

Having a glass of water 15 minutes before eating can help you feel fuller and prevent overeating.

Eat slowly and mindfully

Take your time while eating, chewing thoroughly. This gives your brain time to register that you're full, helping to avoid overindulgence.

Use smaller plates

A smaller plate makes portion control easier. You'll feel like you're eating more without actually consuming extra calories.

Increase your vegetable intake

Fill half your plate with vegetables. They're low in calories, high in fiber, and incredibly filling.

Avoid late-night eating

Try to finish eating 2-3 hours before bed to prevent unnecessary calorie intake and help with digestion.

CHAPTER 3: Energizing Hot Breakfasts

Spinach and Feta Omelette

Prep Time: 5 minutes | Cook Time: 10 minutes | Serves: 2

Ingredients:

- 4 large eggs
- 50 g/2 oz fresh spinach, chopped
- 60 g/2 oz feta cheese, crumbled
- 1 small onion, finely chopped
- 1 tbs olive oil
- Salt and pepper, to taste

Instructions:

1. Heat olive oil in a non-stick skillet over medium heat.
2. Sauté onion for 3-4 minutes until softened.
3. Add spinach and cook for 2 minutes until wilted.
4. Whisk eggs with salt and pepper, then pour into the skillet.
5. Sprinkle the crumbled feta cheese evenly over the omelette.
6. Cook for another 2-3 minutes until the eggs are fully set, and the cheese is slightly melted.
7. Fold the omelette in half and serve immediately.

Nutritional Facts (Per Serving): Calories: 220 kcal | Protein: 15g | Fat: 17g | Carbohydrates: 3g | Fiber: 1g | Sugar: 1g | Sodium: 400mg

Glycemic Index: Low (approximately 15)

Scrambled Eggs with Vegetables

Prep Time: 5 minutes | Cook Time: 10 minutes | Serves: 2

Ingredients:

- 4 large eggs
- 50 g/2 oz bell pepper, diced
- 50 g/2 oz zucchini, diced
- 30g/1 oz onion, finely chopped
- 1 tbsp olive oil
- Salt and pepper, to taste

Instructions:

1. Heat olive oil in a non-stick skillet over medium heat.
2. Sauté onion, bell pepper, and zucchini for 4-5 minutes until softened.
3. Whisk eggs with salt and pepper, then pour into the skillet.
4. Stir gently until eggs are cooked through, about 2-3 minutes.
5. Serve immediately.

Nutritional Facts (Per Serving): Calories: 200 kcal | Protein: 14g | Fat: 15g | Carbohydrates: 5g | Fiber: 1g | Sugar: 2g | Sodium: 300mg

Glycemic Index: Low (approximately 20)

Warm Quinoa Porridge with Berries

Prep Time: 5 minutes | Cook Time: 20 minutes | Serves: 2

Ingredients:

- 100g/3,3 oz quinoa
- 250ml almond milk (unsweetened)
- 50g/2 oz mixed berries
- 1 tsp vanilla extract
- 1/2 tsp cinnamon
- 1/2 tsp stevia or other sugar substitute (optional)

Instructions:

1. Rinse quinoa under cold water.
2. Combine quinoa, almond milk, and vanilla in a saucepan. Bring to a boil.
3. Reduce heat, cover, and simmer for 15 minutes.
4. Stir in cinnamon and stevia, if using.
5. Top with berries and serve warm.

Nutritional Facts (Per Serving): Calories: 300 kcal | Protein: 9g | Fat: 7g | Carbohydrates: 29g | Fiber: 7g | Sugar: 3g | Sodium: 50mg

Glycemic Index: Medium (approximately 50)

Baked Avocado with Egg

Prep Time: 5 minutes | Cook Time: 15 minutes | Serves: 2

Ingredients:

- 1 large avocado, halved and pitted
- 2 large eggs
- Salt and pepper, to taste
- 1 tsp olive oil (optional, for drizzling)
- 1 tsp chopped chives (optional, for garnish)

Instructions:

1. Preheat oven to 190°C (375°F).
2. Scoop out a bit of the avocado flesh to make room for the egg.
3. Place avocado halves in a baking dish. Crack an egg into each half.
4. Season with salt and pepper.
5. Bake for 12-15 minutes until eggs are set.
6. Drizzle with olive oil and garnish with chives, if desired. Serve immediately.

Nutritional Facts (Per Serving): Calories: 280 kcal | Protein: 9g | Fat: 25g | Carbohydrates: 8g | Fiber: 6g | Sugar: 1g | Sodium: 150mg

Glycemic Index: Low (approximately 15)

Tofu Breakfast Burrito

Prep Time: 10 minutes | Cook Time: 15 minutes | Serves: 2

Ingredients:

- 200 g/7 oz firm tofu, crumbled
- 1 small onion, chopped
- 1 small red bell pepper, diced
- 1 small tomato, diced
- 1 tsp olive oil
- 1/2 tsp turmeric
- 1/2 tsp cumin
- Salt and pepper, to taste
- 2 whole grain tortillas
- 1 small avocado, sliced (optional)

Instructions:

1. Heat oil in a skillet over medium heat. Sauté onion and bell pepper for 3-4 minutes.
2. Add tofu, turmeric, cumin, salt, and pepper. Cook for 5-7 minutes until browned.
3. Stir in diced tomato and cook for 2 minutes.
4. Warm tortillas, fill with tofu mixture, and add avocado and cilantro if desired.
5. Roll up burritos and serve warm.

Nutritional Facts (Per Serving): Calories: 320 kcal | Protein: 14g | Fat: 16g | Carbohydrates: 28g | Fiber: 8g | Sugar: 4g | Sodium: 350mg

Glycemic Index: Medium (approximately 50)

Buckwheat Pancakes

Prep Time: 5 minutes | Cook Time: 15 minutes | Serves: 2

Ingredients:

- 100 g/3,3 oz buckwheat flour
- 1 large egg
- 150 ml almond milk (unsweetened)
- 1 tsp baking powder
- 1/2 tsp vanilla extract
- 1/2 tsp cinnamon
- 1 tbsp olive oil (for cooking)
- Optional toppings: fresh berries, Greek yogurt (unsweetened)

Instructions:

1. In a bowl, whisk together buckwheat flour, baking powder, cinnamon, egg, almond milk, and vanilla extract until smooth.
2. Heat olive oil in a non-stick skillet over medium heat.
3. Pour batter onto the skillet, forming small pancakes.
4. Cook for 2-3 minutes on each side until golden brown.
5. Serve warm with optional toppings.

Nutritional Facts (Per Serving): Calories: 300 kcal | Protein: 10g | Fat: 10g | Carbohydrates: 40g | Fiber: 5g | Sugar: 2g | Sodium: 200mg

Glycemic Index: Medium (approximately 50)

Poached Eggs on Whole Grain Toast

Prep Time: 5 minutes | Cook Time: 10 minutes | Serves: 2

Ingredients:

- 2 large eggs
- 2 slices whole grain bread
- 1 tsp vinegar (optional, for poaching)
- Salt and pepper, to taste
- 1 tbsp fresh herbs (e.g., chives or parsley), chopped (optional)

Instructions:

1. Toast the whole grain bread slices to your desired level of crispness.

2. Fill a saucepan with water and bring it to a gentle simmer. Add vinegar to the water if using. Crack each egg into a small bowl, then gently slide the eggs into the simmering water. Poach for 3-4 minutes until the whites are set, and the yolks are still soft.

3. Place a poached egg on each slice of toasted bread. Season with salt and pepper.

4. Sprinkle with fresh herbs if desired, and serve immediately.

Nutritional Facts (Per Serving): Calories: 250 kcal | Protein: 14g | Fat: 10g | Carbohydrates: 22g | Fiber: 4g | Sugar: 2g | Sodium: 300mg

Glycemic Index: Medium (approximately 50)

Oatmeal with Berries and Nuts

Prep Time: 5 minutes | Cook Time: 10 minutes | Serves: 2

Ingredients:

- 80 g/3 oz rolled oats
- 250ml water or unsweetened almond milk
- 50 g/2 oz mixed berries (e.g., blueberries, raspberries)
- 30 g/1 oz mixed nuts, chopped
- 1/2 tsp cinnamon
- 1 tsp vanilla extract
- 1 tsp stevia or another sugar substitute (optional)

Instructions:

1. In a saucepan, bring water or almond milk to a boil. Stir in the oats and reduce the heat to a simmer. Cook for 5-7 minutes until the oats are tender.

2. Stir in the vanilla extract, cinnamon, and stevia (if using).

3. Divide the oatmeal between two bowls. Top with mixed berries and chopped nuts. Serve warm.

Nutritional Facts (Per Serving): Calories: 300 kcal | Protein: 8g | Fat: 12g | Carbohydrates: 35g | Fiber: 7g | Sugar: 5g | Sodium: 100mg

Glycemic Index: Medium (approximately 55)

CHAPTER 4: Refreshing Cold Breakfasts

Overnight Oats with Chia Seeds

Prep Time: 5 minutes | No Cook | Serves: 2

Ingredients:

- 80 g/3 oz rolled oats
- 2 tbsp chia seeds
- 250 ml unsweetened almond milk
- 50 g/2 oz mixed berries
- 1 tsp vanilla extract
- 1 tsp stevia or another sugar substitute (optional)
- 1 tbsp chopped nuts (optional)

Instructions:

1. In a bowl, combine oats, chia seeds, almond milk, vanilla extract, and stevia (if using).
2. Stir the mixture well to ensure all ingredients are evenly distributed.
3. Cover the bowl and refrigerate overnight or for at least 4 hours.
4. In the morning, stir the oats again and divide them between two bowls.
5. Top with mixed berries and chopped nuts, if desired. Serve chilled.

Nutritional Facts (Per Serving): Calories: 250 kcal | Protein: 8g | Fat: 10g | Carbohydrates: 30g | Fiber: 8g | Sugar: 5g | Sodium: 50mg

Glycemic Index: Low (approximately 40)

Cottage Cheese with Fresh Fruit

Prep Time: 5 minutes | No Cook | Serves: 2

Ingredients:

- 200 g/7 oz cottage cheese (low-fat)
- 100 g/3,3 oz fresh fruit (e.g., strawberries, blueberries, or a small apple, diced)
- 1 tbsp chopped nuts (optional)
- 1/2 tsp cinnamon (optional)

Instructions:

1. Divide the cottage cheese evenly between two bowls.
2. Top each serving with fresh fruit.
3. Sprinkle with chopped nuts and cinnamon, if desired.
4. Serve immediately.

Nutritional Facts (Per Serving): Calories: 180 kcal | Protein: 15g | Fat: 6g | Carbohydrates: 14g | Fiber: 2g | Sugar: 10g | Sodium: 400mg

Glycemic Index: Low (approximately 30)

Avocado Toast with Cucumber Slices

Prep Time: 5 minutes | No Cook | Serves: 2

Ingredients:

- 1 large avocado, mashed
- 2 slices whole grain bread
- 1/2 cucumber, thinly sliced
- 1 tsp lemon juice
- Salt and pepper, to taste
- 1 tsp chia seeds (optional)

Instructions:

1. Toast the whole grain bread slices until crispy.
2. In a small bowl, mash the avocado with lemon juice, salt, and pepper.
3. Spread the avocado mixture evenly on each slice of toast.
4. Top with cucumber slices and sprinkle with chia seeds, if desired.
5. Serve immediately.

Nutritional Facts (Per Serving): Calories: 250 kcal | Protein: 6g | Fat: 18g | Carbohydrates: 20g | Fiber: 7g | Sugar: 2g | Sodium: 150mg

Glycemic Index: Low (approximately 40)

Nutty Muesli with Berries

Prep Time: 5 minutes | No Cook | Serves: 2

Ingredients:

- 100 g/3,3 oz rolled oats
- 30 g/1 oz mixed nuts, chopped
- 50 g/2 oz fresh berries (e.g., blueberries, raspberries)
- 1 tbsp chia seeds
- 200ml unsweetened almond milk
- 1 tsp vanilla extract
- 1/2 tsp cinnamon

Instructions:

1. In a bowl, combine rolled oats, mixed nuts, chia seeds, and cinnamon.
2. Stir in almond milk and vanilla extract until well combined.
3. Divide the muesli between two bowls and top with fresh berries.
4. Serve immediately, or let sit for a few minutes to allow the oats to absorb the milk.

Nutritional Facts (Per Serving): Calories: 300 kcal | Protein: 8g | Fat: 15g | Carbohydrates: 30g | Fiber: 8g | Sugar: 5g | Sodium: 50mg

Glycemic Index: Low (approximately 45)

Cold Quinoa Salad with Cucumber and Feta

Prep Time: 10 minutes | Cook Time: 15 minutes (for quinoa) | Serves: 2

Ingredients:

- 100 g/3,3 oz cooked quinoa (cooled)
- 1/2 cucumber, diced
- 50 g/2 oz feta cheese, crumbled
- 1 small red bell pepper, diced
- 1 tbsp olive oil
- 1 tbsp lemon juice
- 1 tbsp fresh parsley, chopped
- Salt and pepper, to taste

Instructions:

1. In a large bowl, combine the cooked quinoa, diced cucumber, red bell pepper, and crumbled feta.
2. In a small bowl, whisk together the olive oil, lemon juice, salt, and pepper.
3. Pour the dressing over the quinoa mixture and toss to combine.
4. Sprinkle with fresh parsley and serve chilled.

Nutritional Facts (Per Serving): Calories: 280 kcal | Protein: 8g | Fat: 16g | Carbohydrates: 25g | Fiber: 4g | Sugar: 3g | Sodium: 300mg

Glycemic Index: Medium (approximately 50)

Smoked Salmon Wraps

Prep Time: 10 minutes | No Cook | Serves: 2

Ingredients:

- 4 slices smoked salmon
- 2 whole grain tortillas
- 50 g/2 oz cream cheese (low-fat)
- 1/2 cucumber, thinly slice
- 1 tbsp fresh dill, chopped
- 1 tbsp capers (optional)
- 1 tsp lemon juice

Instructions:

1. Spread cream cheese evenly over each tortilla.
2. Layer the smoked salmon slices on top of the cream cheese.
3. Add cucumber slices and sprinkle with fresh dill and capers, if using.
4. Drizzle with lemon juice.
5. Roll up the tortillas tightly, slice in half, and serve immediately.

Nutritional Facts (Per Serving): Calories: 280 kcal | Protein: 15g | Fat: 16g | Carbohydrates: 20g | Fiber: 4g | Sugar: 2g | Sodium: 500mg

Glycemic Index: Low (approximately 45)

Chilled Avocado Soup

Prep Time: 10 minutes | No Cook | Serves: 2

Ingredients:

- 2 ripe avocados, peeled and pitted
- 250 ml cold vegetable broth (low-sodium)
- 100 ml unsweetened almond milk
- 2 tbsp fresh lime juice
- 1 small cucumber, peeled and chopped
- 1 small garlic clove, minced
- 1 tbsp fresh cilantro, chopped
- Salt and pepper, to taste
- Lime wedges and cilantro leaves for garnish (optional)

Instructions:

1. In a blender, combine avocados, vegetable broth, almond milk, lime juice, cucumber, and garlic.
2. Blend until smooth and creamy.
3. Season with salt and pepper to taste.
4. Refrigerate for at least 30 minutes before serving.
5. Serve chilled, garnished with lime wedges and cilantro leaves if desired.

Nutritional Facts (Per Serving): Calories: 240 kcal | Protein: 3g | Fat: 20g | Carbohydrates: 14g | Fiber: 9g | Sugar: 3g | Sodium: 150mg

Glycemic Index: Low (approximately 15)

Greek Yogurt Parfait with Nuts

Prep Time: 5 minutes | No Cook | Serves: 2

Ingredients:

- 200 g/7 oz Greek yogurt (unsweetened)
- 50 g/2 oz mixed nuts, chopped
- 1 tsp vanilla extract
- 50 g/7 oz fresh berries (e.g., blueberries, raspberries)
- 1/2 tsp cinnamon

Instructions:

1. In a bowl, mix Greek yogurt with vanilla extract and cinnamon.
2. Layer the yogurt, nuts, and berries in glasses or bowls.
3. Serve the parfaits immediately for a fresh taste, or chill them in the refrigerator for 10-15 minutes before serving if you prefer a colder dessert.

Nutritional Facts (Per Serving): Calories: 300 kcal | Protein: 15g | Fat: 20g | Carbohydrates: 14g | Fiber: 4g | Sugar: 5g | Sodium: 60mg

Glycemic Index: Low (approximately 25)

CHAPTER 5: Nutrient-Packed Smoothies

Apple Cinnamon Smoothie

Prep Time: 5 minutes | No Cook | Serves: 2

Ingredients:

- 1 medium apple, peeled, cored, and chopped
- 150 g/5 oz Greek yogurt (unsweetened)
- 250 ml unsweetened almond milk
- 2 tbsp rolled oats
- 1/2 tsp ground cinnamon
- 1 tsp vanilla extract
- 1/2 tsp stevia or another sugar substitute (optional)
- Ice cubes (optional)

Instructions:

1. In a blender, combine the chopped apple, Greek yogurt, almond milk, rolled oats, cinnamon, vanilla extract, and stevia (if using).
2. Blend until smooth and creamy.
3. If you prefer a colder, thicker smoothie, add a few ice cubes and blend again until smooth.
4. Pour the smoothie into glasses and serve immediately.

Nutritional Facts (Per Serving): Calories: 200 kcal | Protein: 8g | Fat: 4g | Carbohydrates: 30g | Fiber: 4g | Sugar: 12g | Sodium: 60mg

Glycemic Index: Low (approximately 45)

Almond Milk Berry Smoothie

Prep Time: 5 minutes | No Cook | Serves: 2

Ingredients:

- 150 g/5 oz mixed berries (e.g., blueberries, strawberries, raspberries)
- 250 ml unsweetened almond milk
- 50 g/2 oz Greek yogurt (unsweetened)
- 1 tbsp chia seeds
- 1/2 tsp vanilla extract
- 1/2 tsp stevia or another sugar substitute (optional)
- Ice cubes (optional)

Instructions:

1. In a blender, add the mixed berries, almond milk, Greek yogurt, chia seeds, vanilla extract, and stevia (if using).
2. Blend the mixture on high speed until smooth and creamy, ensuring the chia seeds are fully incorporated.
3. If you prefer a thicker smoothie, add a few ice cubes and blend again until smooth.
4. Pour the smoothie into glasses and serve immediately.

Nutritional Facts (Per Serving): Calories: 180 kcal | Protein: 6g | Fat: 7g | Carbohydrates: 22g | Fiber: 8g | Sugar: 10g | Sodium: 50mg

Glycemic Index: Low (approximately 40)

Tropical Green Smoothie

Prep Time: 5 minutes | No Cook | Serves: 2

Ingredients:

- 100 g/3,3 oz fresh spinach
- 150 g/5 oz frozen mango chunks
- 100 g/3,3 oz fresh pineapple chunks
- 250 ml coconut water (unsweetened)
- 1 small banana
- 1 tbsp chia seeds
- 1/2 tsp lime juice
- Ice cubes (optional)

Instructions:

1. In a blender, combine spinach, frozen mango, pineapple, coconut water, banana, chia seeds, and lime juice.
2. Blend on high speed until smooth and creamy.
3. If you prefer a thicker smoothie, add a few ice cubes and blend again until smooth.
4. Pour into glasses and serve immediately.

Nutritional Facts (Per Serving): Calories: 220 kcal | Protein: 4g | Fat: 3g | Carbohydrates: 45g | Fiber: 7g | Sugar: 25g | Sodium: 60mg

Glycemic Index: Medium (approximately 50)

Peanut Butter and Banana Smoothie

Prep Time: 5 minutes | No Cook | Serves: 2

Ingredients:

- 1 large banana
- 2 tbsp peanut butter (unsweetened)
- 250 ml unsweetened almond milk
- 50 g/2 oz Greek yogurt (unsweetened)
- 1 tsp vanilla extract
- Ice cubes (optional)

Instructions:

1. In a blender, combine the banana, peanut butter, almond milk, Greek yogurt, and vanilla extract.
2. Blend until smooth and creamy.
3. If you prefer a thicker smoothie, add a few ice cubes and blend again until smooth.
4. Pour into glasses and serve immediately.

Nutritional Facts (Per Serving): Calories: 300 kcal | Protein: 10g | Fat: 14g | Carbohydrates: 36g | Fiber: 5g | Sugar: 18g | Sodium: 150mg

Glycemic Index: Medium (approximately 50)

Cucumber and Mint Smoothie

Prep Time: 5 minutes | No Cook | Serves: 2

Ingredients:

- 1 large cucumber, peeled and chopped
- 150 g/5 oz Greek yogurt (unsweetened)
- 250 ml unsweetened almond milk
- 1/2 cup fresh mint leaves
- 1 tbsp lime juice
- 1 tsp honey or stevia (optional)
- Ice cubes (optional)

Instructions:

1. In a blender, combine cucumber, Greek yogurt, almond milk, mint leaves, lime juice, and honey or stevia if using.
2. Blend until smooth and creamy.
3. If desired, add ice cubes and blend again for a chilled smoothie.
4. Pour into glasses and serve immediately.

Nutritional Facts (Per Serving): Calories: 120 kcal | Protein: 6g | Fat: 4g | Carbohydrates: 15g | Fiber: 2g | Sugar: 8g | Sodium: 60mg

Glycemic Index: Low (approximately 35)

Avocado and Spinach Smoothie

Prep Time: 5 minutes | No Cook | Serves: 2

Ingredients:

- 1 ripe avocado, peeled and pitted
- 100 g/3,3 oz fresh spinach
- 250 ml unsweetened almond milk
- 1 small banana
- 1 tbsp chia seeds
- 1 tsp honey or stevia (optional)
- Ice cubes (optional)

Instructions:

1. In a blender, combine avocado, spinach, almond milk, banana, chia seeds, and honey or stevia if using.
2. Blend until smooth and creamy.
3. If desired, add ice cubes and blend again until well combined.
4. Pour into glasses and serve immediately.

Nutritional Facts (Per Serving): Calories: 250 kcal | Protein: 4g | Fat: 18g | Carbohydrates: 20g | Fiber: 8g | Sugar: 7g | Sodium: 60mg

Glycemic Index: Low (approximately 35)

Pumpkin Spice Smoothie

Prep Time: 5 minutes | No Cook | Serves: 2

Ingredients:

- 150 g/5 oz pumpkin puree (unsweetened)
- 250 ml unsweetened almond milk
- 50 g/2 oz Greek yogurt (unsweetened)
- 1 small banana
- 1 tsp pumpkin spice blend
- 1/2 tsp vanilla extract
- 1 tsp honey or stevia (optional)
- Ice cubes (optional)

Instructions:

1. In a blender, combine pumpkin puree, almond milk, Greek yogurt, banana, pumpkin spice, vanilla extract, and honey or stevia if using.
2. Blend until smooth and creamy.
3. If desired, add ice cubes and blend again until well combined.
4. Pour into glasses and serve immediately.

Nutritional Facts (Per Serving): Calories: 180 kcal | Protein: 6g | Fat: 4g | Carbohydrates: 30g | Fiber: 5g | Sugar: 12g | Sodium: 60mg

Glycemic Index: Low (approximately 45)

Green Detox Smoothie

Prep Time: 5 minutes | No Cook | Serves: 2

Ingredients:

- 100 g/3,3 oz fresh spinach
- 1 small cucumber, peeled and chopped
- 1 small green apple, cored and chopped
- 1 small lemon, juiced
- 250 ml coconut water (unsweetened)
- 1 tbsp chia seeds
- 1/2 tsp grated fresh ginger (optional)
- Ice cubes (optional)

Instructions:

1. In a blender, combine spinach, cucumber, green apple, lemon juice, coconut water, chia seeds, and grated ginger if using.
2. Blend until smooth and creamy.
3. If desired, add ice cubes and blend again until well combined.
4. Pour into glasses and serve immediately.

Nutritional Facts (Per Serving): Calories: 120 kcal | Protein: 3g | Fat: 2g | Carbohydrates: 25g | Fiber: 7g | Sugar: 15g | Sodium: 50mg

Glycemic Index: Low (approximately 30)

CHAPTER 6: Vibrant Fresh Salads

Mediterranean Quinoa Salad

Prep Time: 10 minutes | Cook Time: 15 minutes (for quinoa) | Serves: 2

Ingredients:

- 100 g/3,3 oz quinoa, rinsed
- 200 ml water
- 50 g/2 oz cherry tomatoes, halved
- 50 g/2 oz cucumber, diced
- 30 g/1 oz Kalamata olives, pitted and sliced
- 1 tbsp red onion, finely chopped
- 1 tbsp fresh parsley, chopped
- 1 tbsp extra virgin olive oil
- 1 tbsp lemon juice
- Salt and pepper, to taste

Instructions:

1. In a saucepan, bring water to a boil. Add quinoa, reduce heat to low, cover, and simmer for 15 minutes or until quinoa is tender and water is absorbed. Fluff with a fork and let cool.
2. In a large bowl, mix quinoa with tomatoes, cucumber, olives, feta, onion, and parsley.
3. Whisk together olive oil, lemon juice, salt, and pepper. Toss with salad.
4. Serve immediately, or chill for 2 hours.

Nutritional Facts (Per Serving): Calories: 280 kcal | Protein: 8g | Fat: 14g | Carbohydrates: 28g | Fiber: 5g | Sugar: 4g | Sodium: 400mg

Glycemic Index: Medium (approximately 50)

Cucumber and Avocado Salad with Lemon Dressing

Prep Time: 10 minutes | No Cook | Serves: 2

Ingredients:

- 1 large cucumber, diced
- 1 ripe avocado, diced
- 1 tbsp fresh lemon juice
- 1 tbsp extra virgin olive oi
- 1 tbsp fresh parsley, chopped
- Salt and pepper, to taste

Instructions:

1. In a large bowl, combine diced cucumber and avocado.
2. In a small bowl, whisk together lemon juice, olive oil, salt, and pepper.
3. Pour the dressing over the cucumber and avocado, tossing gently to combine.
4. Sprinkle with fresh parsley and serve immediately.

Nutritional Facts (Per Serving): Calories: 220 kcal | Protein: 2g | Fat: 19g | Carbohydrates: 12g | Fiber: 7g | Sugar: 3g | Sodium: 10mg

Glycemic Index: Low (approximately 20)

Spinach and Strawberry Salad

Prep Time: 10 minutes | No Cook | Serves: 2

Ingredients:

- 100 g/3,3 oz fresh spinach leaves
- 150 g/5 oz strawberries, sliced
- 2 tbsp sliced almonds, toasted
- 30 g/1 oz feta cheese, crumbled
- 1 tbsp balsamic vinegar
- 1 tbsp extra virgin olive oil
- Salt and pepper, to taste

Instructions:

1. In a large bowl, combine spinach, sliced strawberries, and crumbled feta cheese.
2. In a small bowl, whisk together balsamic vinegar, olive oil, salt, and pepper.
3. Drizzle the dressing over the salad and toss gently to combine.
4. Sprinkle with toasted almonds and serve immediately.

Nutritional Facts (Per Serving): Calories: 200 kcal | Protein: 6g | Fat: 14g | Carbohydrates: 15g | Fiber: 4g | Sugar: 8g | Sodium: 200mg

Glycemic Index: Low (approximately 30)

Greek Salad with Feta and Olives

Prep Time: 10 minutes | No Cook | Serves: 2

Ingredients:

- 100 g/3,3 oz cherry tomatoes, halved
- 1 small cucumber, diced
- 1/2 red onion, thinly sliced
- 50 g/2 oz Kalamata olives, pitted
- 50 g/2 oz feta cheese, crumbled
- 1 tbsp extra virgin olive oil
- 1 tbsp red wine vinegar
- 1 tsp dried oregano
- Salt and pepper, to taste

Instructions:

1. In a large bowl, combine cherry tomatoes, cucumber, red onion, olives, and feta cheese.
2. In a small bowl, whisk together olive oil, red wine vinegar, oregano, salt, and pepper.
3. Pour the dressing over the salad and toss gently to combine.
4. Serve immediately.

Nutritional Facts (Per Serving): Calories: 250 kcal | Protein: 6g | Fat: 20g | Carbohydrates: 12g | Fiber: 3g | Sugar: 5g | Sodium: 450mg

Glycemic Index: Low (approximately 35)

Roasted Beet and Goat Cheese Salad

Prep Time: 10 minutes | Cook Time: 40 minutes (for roasting beets) | Serves: 2

Ingredients:

- 2 medium beets, roasted, peeled, and diced
- 50 g/2 oz goat cheese, crumbled
- 50 g/2 oz mixed greens (e.g., spinach, arugula)
- 1 tbsp balsamic vinegar
- 2 tbsp walnuts, toasted and chopped
- 1 tbsp extra virgin olive oil
- 1 tsp honey or stevia (optional)
- Salt and pepper to taste

Instructions:

1. Preheat the oven to 200°C (400°F). Wrap each beet in foil and roast for 40 minutes, or until tender. Let cool, then peel and dice the beets.
2. In a large bowl, combine roasted beets, mixed greens, crumbled goat cheese, and toasted walnuts.
3. In a small bowl, whisk together balsamic vinegar, olive oil, honey or stevia (if using), salt, and pepper.
4. Drizzle the dressing over the salad and toss gently to combine.
5. Serve immediately.

Nutritional Facts (Per Serving): Calories: 280 kcal | Protein: 7g | Fat: 18g | Carbohydrates: 22g | Fiber: 6g | Sugar: 13g | Sodium: 250mg

Glycemic Index: Medium (approximately 50)

Kale and Apple Salad with Walnuts

Prep Time: 10 minutes | No Cook | Serves: 2

Ingredients:

- 100 g/3,3 oz kale, stems removed and leaves chopped
- 1 medium apple, cored and thinly sliced
- 30 g/1 oz walnuts, toasted and chopped
- 30 g/1 oz feta cheese, crumbled (optional)
- 1 tbsp lemon juice
- 1 tbsp extra virgin olive oil
- 1 tsp honey or stevia (optional)
- Salt and pepper, to taste

Instructions:

1. In a large bowl, combine chopped kale, apple slices, walnuts, and feta cheese (if using).
2. In a small bowl, whisk together lemon juice, olive oil, honey or stevia (if using), salt, and pepper.
3. Pour the dressing over the salad and toss to combine.
4. Serve immediately.

Nutritional Facts (Per Serving): Calories: 220 kcal | Protein: 5g | Fat: 16g | Carbohydrates: 18g | Fiber: 4g | Sugar: 10g | Sodium: 150mg

Glycemic Index: Low (approximately 30)

Chicken Caesar Salad

Prep Time: 10 minutes | Cook Time: 15 minutes | Serves: 2

Ingredients:

- 200 g/7 oz chicken breast, cooked and sliced
- 100 g/3,3 oz romaine lettuce, chopped
- 30 g/1 oz Parmesan cheese, grated
- 30 g/1 oz whole grain croutons
- 2 tbsp Caesar dressing (low-fat)
- 1 tbsp fresh lemon juice
- Salt and pepper, to taste

Instructions:

1. In a large bowl, combine chopped romaine lettuce, sliced chicken breast, Parmesan cheese, and croutons.
2. Drizzle the Caesar dressing and lemon juice over the salad.
3. Toss gently to combine, ensuring the salad is evenly coated with dressing.
4. Season with salt and pepper to taste, and serve immediately.

Nutritional Facts (Per Serving): Calories: 320 kcal | Protein: 30g | Fat: 14g | Carbohydrates: 15g | Fiber: 3g | Sugar: 2g | Sodium: 550mg

Glycemic Index: Low (approximately 45)

Tuna Salad with Avocado

Prep Time: 10 minutes | No Cook | Serves: 2

Ingredients:

- 1 large avocado, diced
- 1 can (150 g/5 oz) tuna in water, drained
- 1 small cucumber, diced
- 1 tbsp red onion, finely chopped
- 1 tbsp fresh lemon juice
- 1 tbsp extra virgin olive oil
- 1 tbsp fresh parsley, chopped
- Salt and pepper, to taste

Instructions:

1. In a large bowl, combine diced avocado, drained tuna, cucumber, and red onion.
2. In a small bowl, whisk together lemon juice, olive oil, salt, and pepper.
3. Pour the dressing over the salad and toss gently to combine.
4. Sprinkle with fresh parsley and serve immediately.

Nutritional Facts (Per Serving): Calories: 280 kcal | Protein: 20g | Fat: 18g | Carbohydrates: 8g | Fiber: 5g | Sugar: 2g | Sodium: 300mg

Glycemic Index: Low (approximately 25)

CHAPTER 7: Wholesome Wraps and Sandwiches

Grilled Chicken and Avocado Wrap

Prep Time: 10 minutes | Cook Time: 15 minutes | Serves: 2

Ingredients:

- 200 g/7 oz chicken breast, grilled and sliced
- 1 large avocado, sliced
- 2 whole grain tortillas
- 50 g/2 oz lettuce leaves
- 1 small tomato, sliced
- 2 tbsp Greek yogurt (unsweetened)
- 1 tbsp fresh lemon juice
- Salt and pepper, to taste

Instructions:

1. Lay the tortillas flat and spread Greek yogurt evenly over each.
2. Layer the lettuce, grilled chicken, avocado slices, and tomato slices on each tortilla.
3. Drizzle with lemon juice and season with salt and pepper.
4. Roll up the tortillas tightly, slice in half, and serve immediately.

Nutritional Facts (Per Serving): Calories: 350 kcal | Protein: 28g | Fat: 18g | Carbohydrates: 25g | Fiber: 8g | Sugar: 3g | Sodium: 350mg

Glycemic Index: Medium (approximately 50)

Turkey and Spinach Whole Grain Sandwich

Prep Time: 10 minutes | No Cook | Serves: 2

Ingredients:

- 4 slices whole grain bread
- 200 g/7 oz sliced turkey breast (cooked)
- 50 g/2 oz fresh spinach leaves
- 1 small tomato, sliced
- 2 tbsp Dijon mustard
- 1 tbsp light mayonnaise (optional)
- Salt and pepper, to taste

Instructions:

1. Spread Dijon mustard on two slices of whole grain bread. If using, spread light mayonnaise on the other two slices.
2. Layer turkey breast slices, spinach leaves, and tomato slices on two slices of bread.
3. Season with salt and pepper to taste.
4. Top with the remaining slices of bread, cut in half, and serve immediately.

Nutritional Facts (Per Serving): Calories: 300 kcal | Protein: 25g | Fat: 8g | Carbohydrates: 32g | Fiber: 6g | Sugar: 4g | Sodium: 600mg

Glycemic Index: Medium (approximately 50)

Tuna Salad Lettuce Wraps

Prep Time: 10 minutes | No Cook | Serves: 2

Ingredients:

- 1 can (150 g/5 oz) tuna in water, drained
- 1 small avocado, diced
- 1 tbsp Greek yogurt (unsweetened
- 1 tbsp fresh lemon juice
- 1 tbsp fresh parsley, chopped
- 4 large lettuce leaves (e.g., romaine or iceberg)
- Salt and pepper, to taste

Instructions:

1. In a medium bowl, combine drained tuna, diced avocado, Greek yogurt, lemon juice, parsley, salt, and pepper. Mix until well combined.
2. Place a spoonful of the tuna salad mixture onto each lettuce leaf.
3. Fold or roll the lettuce leaves around the filling to form wraps.
4. Serve immediately.

Nutritional Facts (Per Serving): Calories: 220 kcal | Protein: 20g | Fat: 14g | Carbohydrates: 5g | Fiber: 3g | Sugar: 1g | Sodium: 250mg

Glycemic Index: Low (approximately 25)

Hummus and Veggie Pita Wrap

Prep Time: 10 minutes | No Cook | Serves: 2

Ingredients:

- 2 whole grain pita breads
- 100 g/3,3 oz hummus
- 50 g/2 oz fresh spinach leaves
- 1 small cucumber, sliced
- 1 small red bell pepper, sliced
- 1 small carrot, grated
- 1 tbsp lemon juice
- Salt and pepper, to taste

Instructions:

1. Slice the pita breads in half to create pockets.
2. Spread hummus evenly inside each pita pocket.
3. Stuff the pita pockets with spinach, cucumber, bell pepper, and grated carrot.
4. Drizzle with lemon juice and season with salt and pepper.
5. Serve immediately.

Nutritional Facts (Per Serving): Calories: 300 kcal | Protein: 10g | Fat: 10g | Carbohydrates: 40g | Fiber: 8g | Sugar: 5g | Sodium: 350mg

Glycemic Index: Medium (approximately 50)

Smoked Salmon and Cream Cheese Sandwich

Prep Time: 10 minutes | No Cook | Serves: 2

Ingredients:

- 4 slices whole grain bread
- 100 g/3,3 oz smoked salmon
- 50 g/2 oz cream cheese (low-fat)
- 1 small cucumber, thinly slice
- 1 tbsp fresh dill, chopped
- 1 tsp lemon juice
- Salt and pepper, to taste

Instructions:

1. Spread cream cheese evenly over two slices of whole grain bread.
2. Layer smoked salmon and cucumber slices on top of the cream cheese.
3. Sprinkle with chopped dill, drizzle with lemon juice, and season with salt and pepper.
4. Top with the remaining slices of bread, cut in half, and serve immediately.

Nutritional Facts (Per Serving): Calories: 300 kcal | Protein: 15g | Fat: 12g | Carbohydrates: 30g | Fiber: 6g | Sugar: 3g | Sodium: 500mg

Glycemic Index: Low (approximately 45)

Egg Salad Lettuce Wrap

Prep Time: 10 minutes | No Cook | Serves: 2

Ingredients:

- 4 large eggs, hard-boiled and chopped
- 2 tbsp Greek yogurt (unsweetened)
- 1 tbsp Dijon mustard
- 1 tbsp fresh chives, chopped
- 1 tbsp fresh parsley, chopped
- 4 large lettuce leaves (e.g., romaine or iceberg)
- Salt and pepper, to taste

Instructions:

1. In a medium bowl, combine chopped eggs, Greek yogurt, Dijon mustard, chives, parsley, salt, and pepper. Mix until well combined.
2. Place a spoonful of the egg salad mixture onto each lettuce leaf.
3. Fold or roll the lettuce leaves around the filling to form wraps.
4. Serve immediately.

Nutritional Facts (Per Serving): Calories: 220 kcal | Protein: 14g | Fat: 16g | Carbohydrates: 3g | Fiber: 1g | Sugar: 1g | Sodium: 250mg

Glycemic Index: Low (approximately 25)

Roast Beef and Arugula Sandwich

Prep Time: 10 minutes | No Cook | Serves: 2

Ingredients:

- 4 slices whole grain bread
- 150 g/5 oz roast beef, thinly sliced
- 50 g/2 oz fresh arugula
- 1 small tomato, sliced
- 2 tbsp Dijon mustard
- 1 tbsp horseradish sauce (optional)
- Salt and pepper, to taste

Instructions:

1. Spread Dijon mustard on two slices of whole grain bread. If using, spread horseradish sauce on the other two slices.
2. Layer roast beef slices, arugula, and tomato slices on two slices of bread.
3. Season with salt and pepper to taste.
4. Top with the remaining slices of bread, cut in half, and serve immediately.

Nutritional Facts (Per Serving): Calories: 320 kcal | Protein: 22g | Fat: 10g | Carbohydrates: 34g | Fiber: 6g | Sugar: 4g | Sodium: 600mg

Glycemic Index: Medium (approximately 50)

BLT Wrap with Turkey Bacon

Prep Time: 10 minutes | Cook Time: 10 minutes | Serves: 2

Ingredients:

- 4 slices turkey bacon
- 2 whole grain tortillas
- 50 g/2 oz lettuce leaves
- 1 small tomato, sliced
- 2 tbsp light mayonnaise (optional)
- 1 tbsp Dijon mustard (optional)
- Salt and pepper, to taste

Instructions:

1. Cook turkey bacon in a skillet over medium heat until crispy, about 5 minutes per side. Drain on paper towels.
2. Lay the tortillas flat and spread mayonnaise and Dijon mustard evenly over each, if using.
3. Layer lettuce leaves, tomato slices, and turkey bacon on each tortilla.
4. Season with salt and pepper to taste.
5. Roll up the tortillas tightly, slice in half, and serve immediately.

Nutritional Facts (Per Serving): Calories: 280 kcal | Protein: 15g | Fat: 12g | Carbohydrates: 28g | Fiber: 5g | Sugar: 3g | Sodium: 550mg

Glycemic Index: Low (approximately 45)

CHAPTER 8: Comforting Soups and Stews

Lentil and Vegetable Soup

Prep Time: 10 minutes | Cook Time: 30 minutes | Serves: 2

Ingredients:

- 100 g/3,3 oz dried lentils, rinsed
- 1 small onion, chopped
- 1 small carrot, diced
- 1 celery stalk, diced
- 2 garlic cloves, minced
- 400 ml vegetable broth (low-sodium)
- 1 tbsp olive oil
- 200 g/7 oz diced tomatoes (canned, no added salt)
- 1 tsp ground cumin
- 1/2 tsp dried thyme
- Salt and pepper, to taste
- 1 tbsp fresh parsley, chopped (optional)

Instructions:

1. In a large pot, heat olive oil over medium heat. Add chopped onion, carrot, celery, and garlic. Sauté for 5-7 minutes until vegetables are softened.
2. Add rinsed lentils, vegetable broth, diced tomatoes, cumin, and thyme. Bring to a boil.
3. Reduce heat to low, cover, and simmer for 25-30 minutes until lentils are tender.
4. Season with salt and pepper to taste. Stir in fresh parsley if using. Serve hot.

Nutritional Facts (Per Serving): Calories: 250 kcal | Protein: 12g | Fat: 7g | Carbohydrates: 35g | Fiber: 12g | Sugar: 8g | Sodium: 300m

Glycemic Index: Low (approximately 30)

Chicken and Kale Stew

Prep Time: 10 minutes | Cook Time: 30 minutes | Serves: 2

Ingredients:

- 200 g/7 oz chicken breast, diced
- 1 small onion, chopped
- 2 garlic cloves, minced
- 1 small carrot, sliced
- 1 celery stalk, diced
- 1 tbsp olive oil
- 150 g/5 oz kale, stems removed and chopped
- 400 ml chicken broth (low-sodium)
- 1 tsp dried thyme
- 1 tsp dried oregano
- Salt and pepper, to taste

Instructions:

1. Heat olive oil in a pot over medium heat. Add chicken, onion, and garlic. Cook until chicken is browned and onion is softened.
2. Add carrot and celery, and cook for another 3-4 minutes.
3. Pour in chicken broth and stir in thyme, oregano, salt, and pepper. Bring to a boil.
4. Reduce heat, cover, and simmer for 20 minutes.
5. Add kale, stir, and cook for 5 minutes until wilted. Serve hot.

Nutritional Facts (Per Serving): Calories: 280 kcal | Protein: 28g | Fat: 10g | Carbohydrates: 20g | Fiber: 6g | Sugar: 5g | Sodium: 400mg

Glycemic Index: Low (approximately 35)

Tomato Basil Soup

Prep Time: 10 minutes | Cook Time: 20 minutes | Serves: 2

Ingredients:

- 400 g/14 oz canned diced tomatoes (no added salt)
- 1 small onion, chopped
- 2 garlic cloves, minced
- 1 tbsp olive oil
- 200 ml vegetable broth (low-sodium)
- 1 tbsp tomato paste
- 1 tsp dried basil (or 1/4 cup fresh basil leaves, chopped)
- 1/2 tsp dried oregano
- Salt and pepper, to taste
- 1 tbsp fresh basil leaves, chopped (for garnish)

Instructions:

1. In a large pot, heat olive oil over medium heat. Add chopped onion and garlic. Sauté for 5-7 minutes until the onion is softened.
2. Add diced tomatoes (with their juice), vegetable broth, tomato paste, dried basil, and oregano. Stir to combine.
3. Bring the soup to a boil, then reduce heat to low and simmer for 15-20 minutes.
4. If using fresh basil, stir it in during the last 5 minutes of cooking.
5. Use an immersion blender to puree the soup until smooth, or leave it chunky if you prefer.
6. Season with salt and pepper to taste. Garnish with fresh basil leaves if desired, and serve hot.

Nutritional Facts (Per Serving): Calories: 180 kcal | Protein: 4g | Fat: 7g | Carbohydrates: 26g | Fiber: 6g | Sugar: 14g | Sodium: 300mg

Glycemic Index: Low (approximately 30)

Butternut Squash Soup

Prep Time: 10 minutes | Cook Time: 25 minutes | Serves: 2

Ingredients:

- 400 g/14 oz butternut squash, peeled and cubed
- 1 small onion, chopped
- 2 garlic cloves, minced
- 1 tbsp olive oil
- 1/2 tsp ground cinnamon
- 400 ml vegetable broth (low-sodium)
- 1/4 tsp ground nutmeg (optional)
- Salt and pepper, to taste
- 1 tbsp Greek yogurt (for garnish, optional)

Instructions:

1. Heat olive oil in a pot over medium heat. Sauté onion and garlic until softened, about 5 minutes.
2. Add butternut squash cubes and cook for 5 minutes, stirring occasionally.
3. Pour in vegetable broth, add cinnamon, and nutmeg if using. Bring to a boil.
4. Reduce heat, cover, and simmer for 15-20 minutes until the squash is tender.
5. Puree the soup with an immersion blender until smooth.
6. Season with salt and pepper. Garnish with a dollop of Greek yogurt if desired, and serve hot.

Nutritional Facts (Per Serving): Calories: 180 kcal | Protein: 3g | Fat: 7g | Carbohydrates: 28g | Fiber: 5g | Sugar: 8g | Sodium: 300mg

Glycemic Index: Low (approximately 30)

Zucchini and Leek Soup

Prep Time: 10 minutes | Cook Time: 20 minutes | Serves: 2

Ingredients:

- 2 medium zucchinis, chopped
- 1 large leek, white and light green parts only, sliced
- 2 garlic cloves, minced
- 1 tbsp olive oil
- 400 ml vegetable broth (low-sodium)
- 1 tsp dried thyme
- Salt and pepper, to taste
- 1 tbsp fresh parsley, chopped (optional, for garnish)

Instructions:

1. Heat olive oil in a pot over medium heat. Sauté sliced leek and garlic until softened, about 5 minutes.
2. Add chopped zucchini and cook for another 3-4 minutes.
3. Pour in vegetable broth and stir in dried thyme. Bring to a boil.
4. Reduce heat, cover, and simmer for 15 minutes until the zucchini is tender.
5. Puree the soup with an immersion blender until smooth, or leave it chunky if preferred.
6. Season with salt and pepper. Garnish with fresh parsley if desired, and serve hot.

Nutritional Facts (Per Serving): Calories: 150 kcal | Protein: 4g | Fat: 7g | Carbohydrates: 18g | Fiber: 4g | Sugar: 9g | Sodium: 300mg

Glycemic Index: Low (approximately 30)

Moroccan Chickpea Stew

Prep Time: 10 minutes | Cook Time: 30 minutes | Serves: 2

Ingredients:

- 1 can (400g/14 oz) chickpeas, drained and rinsed
- 1 small onion, chopped
- 2 garlic cloves, minced
- 1 small carrot, diced
- 1 small zucchini, diced
- 400 g/14 oz canned diced tomatoes (no added salt)
- 1 tbsp olive oil
- 200 ml vegetable broth (low-sodium)
- 1 tsp ground cumin
- 1/2 tsp ground coriander
- 1/2 tsp ground cinnamon
- 1/4 tsp ground turmeric
- 1 tbsp fresh cilantro, chopped (optional, for garnish)
- Salt and pepper, to taste

Instructions:

1. Heat olive oil in a pot over medium heat. Sauté onion, garlic, and carrot until softened, about 5 minutes.
2. Add zucchini and cook for another 3 minutes.
3. Stir in chickpeas, diced tomatoes, vegetable broth, cumin, coriander, cinnamon, and turmeric. Bring to a boil.
4. Reduce heat, cover, and simmer for 20 minutes until the vegetables are tender and the flavors meld.
5. Season with salt and pepper to taste. Garnish with fresh cilantro if desired, and serve hot.

Nutritional Facts (Per Serving): Calories: 280 kcal | Protein: 10g | Fat: 8g | Carbohydrates: 42g | Fiber: 10g | Sugar: 10g | Sodium: 400mg

Glycemic Index: Low (approximately 35)

Beef and Barley Soup

Prep Time: 10 minutes | Cook Time: 40 minutes | Serves: 2

Ingredients:

- 200 g/7 oz beef stew meat, cubed
- 1 small onion, chopped
- 2 garlic cloves, minced
- 1 small carrot, sliced
- 1 celery stalk, diced
- 1/2 cup (100g) pearl barley, rinsed
- 1 tbsp olive oil
- 600 ml beef broth (low-sodium)
- 1 bay leaf
- 1 tsp dried thyme
- Salt and pepper, to taste
- Fresh parsley, chopped (optional, for garnish)

Instructions:

1. Heat olive oil in a large pot over medium heat. Add beef cubes and brown on all sides, about 5 minutes.
2. Add onion, garlic, carrot, and celery. Sauté for 5 minutes until vegetables are softened.
3. Stir in barley, beef broth, bay leaf, and thyme. Bring to a boil.
4. Reduce heat, cover, and simmer for 30-35 minutes until barley and beef are tender.
5. Remove bay leaf. Season with salt and pepper to taste. Garnish with fresh parsley if desired, and serve hot.

Nutritional Facts (Per Serving): Calories: 350 kcal | Protein: 22g | Fat: 12g | Carbohydrates: 38g | Fiber: 8g | Sugar: 4g | Sodium: 500mg

Glycemic Index: Medium (approximately 50)

Minestrone with White Beans

Prep Time: 10 minutes | Cook Time: 30 minutes | Serves: 2

Ingredients:

- 1 small onion, chopped
- 2 garlic cloves, minced
- 1 small carrot, diced
- 1 celery stalk, diced
- 1 small zucchini, diced
- 1 can (400g/14 oz) diced tomatoes (no added salt)
- 600 ml vegetable broth (low-sodium)
- 1 can (400 g/14 oz) white beans, drained and rinsed
- 1/2 tsp dried oregano
- 1/2 tsp dried basil
- 1 bay leaf
- Salt and pepper, to taste
- 1 tbsp fresh parsley, chopped (optional, for garnish)

Instructions:

1. In a large pot, heat olive oil over medium heat. Sauté onion, garlic, carrot, and celery for 5-7 minutes until softened.
2. Add zucchini, diced tomatoes, white beans, vegetable broth, oregano, basil, and bay leaf. Stir to combine.
3. Bring the soup to a boil, then reduce heat and simmer for 20-25 minutes until vegetables are tender.
4. Remove bay leaf. Season with salt and pepper to taste. Garnish with fresh parsley if desired, and serve hot.

Nutritional Facts (Per Serving): Calories: 280 kcal | Protein: 10g | Fat: 4g | Carbohydrates: 48g | Fiber: 12g | Sugar: 10g | Sodium: 350mg

Glycemic Index: Low (approximately 40)

CHAPTER 9: Protein-Packed Main Courses

Grilled Chicken Breasts

Prep Time: 10 minutes | Cook Time: 15 minutes | Serves: 2

Ingredients:

- 2 boneless, skinless chicken breasts (200 g/7 oz each)
- 2 tbsp olive oil
- 1 tbsp lemon juice
- 1 tsp dried oregano
- 1 tsp dried thyme
- 1 tsp garlic powder
- Salt and pepper, to taste

Instructions:

1. Mix olive oil, lemon juice, oregano, thyme, garlic powder, salt, and pepper in a bowl.
2. Place chicken breasts in a resealable bag or shallow dish. Pour the marinade over the chicken, ensuring it is well coated. Marinate for at least 30 minutes, or up to 2 hours in the refrigerator.
3. Grill the chicken for 6-7 minutes on each side, or until the internal temperature reaches 75°C (165°F) and the chicken is fully cooked.
4. Let rest, then slice and serve.

Nutritional Facts (Per Serving): Calories: 300 kcal | Protein: 35g | Fat: 16g | Carbohydrates: 1g | Fiber: 0g | Sugar: 0g | Sodium: 200mg

Glycemic Index: Low (approximately 20)

Turkey Burgers with Portobello Mushroom Buns

Prep Time: 10 minutes | Cook Time: 25 minutes | Serves: 2

Ingredients:

- 250 g/9 oz lean ground turkey
- 2 tbsp fresh parsley, chopped
- 1 garlic clove, minced
- 1 tsp olive oil
- 1 tsp dried oregano
- Salt and pepper to taste
- 4 large Portobello mushroom caps
- For topping, optional: tomato, avocado, lettuce

Instructions:

1. Preheat oven to 375°F (190°C). Season mushroom caps with olive oil, salt, and pepper. Bake gill side up for 10–12 minutes.
2. Mix ground turkey with parsley, garlic, oregano, salt, and pepper. Form into patties.
3. Cook patties in a skillet over medium heat for 5–6 minutes on each side until fully cooked.
4. Assemble burgers with mushroom caps, turkey patties, and optional toppings like lettuce, tomato, or avocado.
5. Serve immediately.

Nutritional Facts (Per Serving): Calories: 350 kcal | Protein: 36g | Fat: 18g | Carbohydrates: 10g | Fiber: 2g | Sugar: 4g | Sodium: 400mg

Glycemic Index: Low (approximately 15)

Beef Stir-Fry with Broccoli

Prep Time: 10 minutes | Cook Time: 15 minutes | Serves: 2

Ingredients:

- 200 g/7 oz beef sirloin, thinly sliced
- 1 small head of broccoli, cut into florets
- 1 small onion, sliced
- 2 garlic cloves, minced
- 1 tbsp soy sauce (low-sodium)
- 1 tbsp olive oil
- 1 tsp sesame oil
- 1 tsp fresh ginger, grated
- Salt and pepper, to taste
- 1 tbsp sesame seeds (for garnish)

Instructions:

1. Heat olive oil in a large skillet or wok over medium-high heat. Add the sliced beef and cook for 3-4 minutes until browned. Remove and set aside.
2. In the same skillet, add the onion, garlic, and ginger. Sauté for 2 minutes until fragrant.
3. Add the broccoli florets and stir-fry for 5-7 minutes until tender-crisp.
4. Return the beef to the skillet, add soy sauce and sesame oil. Stir well and cook for an additional 2-3 minutes.
5. Season with salt and pepper to taste. Garnish with sesame seeds if desired, and serve hot.

Nutritional Facts (Per Serving): Calories: 300 kcal | Protein: 25g | Fat: 18g | Carbohydrates: 10g | Fiber: 4g | Sugar: 3g | Sodium: 400mg

Glycemic Index: Low (approximately 30)

Turkey Meatballs with Tomato Sauce

Prep Time: 10 minutes | Cook Time: 25 minutes | Serves: 2

Ingredients:

- 200 g/7 oz ground turkey
- 1 small onion, finely chopped
- 2 garlic cloves, minced
- 1/4 cup breadcrumbs (whole grain)
- 1 egg, beaten
- 1 tbsp fresh parsley, chopped
- 1 tsp dried oregano
- Salt and pepper, to taste
- 1 tbsp olive oil
- 200 g/7 oz canned diced tomatoes (no added salt)
- 1 tbsp tomato paste
- 1 tsp dried basil

Instructions:

1. Mix turkey, onion, half the garlic, breadcrumbs, egg, parsley, oregano, salt, and pepper. Form meatballs.
2. Heat olive oil in a skillet. Brown meatballs on all sides, about 5-7 minutes, turning occasionally, until browned on all sides.
3. Add remaining garlic, tomatoes, tomato paste, and basil. Stir gently to combine. Reduce heat, cover, and simmer for 15-20 minutes until the meatballs are cooked through and the sauce has thickened.
4. Serve hot, garnished with additional parsley if desired.

Nutritional Facts (Per Serving): Calories: 320 kcal | Protein: 28g | Fat: 16g | Carbohydrates: 18g | Fiber: 4g | Sugar: 6g | Sodium: 400mg

Glycemic Index: Low (approximately 35)

Pork Tenderloin with Green Beans

Prep Time: 10 minutes | Cook Time: 20 minutes | Serves: 2

Ingredients:

- 200 g/7 oz pork tenderloin, sliced into medallions
- 200 g/7 oz green beans, trimmed
- 2 garlic cloves, minced
- 1 tbsp olive oil
- 1 tbsp soy sauce (low-sodium)
- 1 tsp Dijon mustard
- Salt and pepper, to taste
- 1 tsp fresh thyme leaves (optional)

Instructions:

1. Heat olive oil in a large skillet over medium heat. Add the pork medallions and cook for 3-4 minutes per side until browned. Remove from skillet and set aside.
2. In the same skillet, add minced garlic and green beans. Sauté for 5-7 minutes until green beans are tender-crisp.
3. Return the pork to the skillet. Add soy sauce, Dijon mustard, salt, pepper, and thyme if using. Cook for an additional 3-4 minutes until the pork is fully cooked and the flavors meld.
4. Serve hot.

Nutritional Facts (Per Serving): Calories: 320 kcal | Protein: 28g | Fat: 16g | Carbohydrates: 10g | Fiber: 4g | Sugar: 3g | Sodium: 450mg

Glycemic Index: Low (approximately 30)

Baked Chicken with Rosemary and Garlic

Prep Time: 10 minutes | Cook Time: 25 minutes | Serves: 2

Ingredients:

- 2 boneless, skinless chicken breasts (approximately 200 g/7 oz each)
- 2 garlic cloves, minced
- 1 tbsp fresh rosemary, chopped
- 2 tbsp olive oil
- 1 tbsp lemon juice
- Salt and pepper, to taste

Instructions:

1. Preheat the oven to 200°C (400°F).
2. In a small bowl, mix together minced garlic, rosemary, olive oil, lemon juice, salt, and pepper.
3. Rub the mixture over the chicken breasts, coating them evenly.
4. Place the chicken in a baking dish and bake for 20-25 minutes, or until the internal temperature reaches 75°C (165°F) and the chicken is fully cooked.
5. Let rest for a few minutes before serving.

Nutritional Facts (Per Serving): Calories: 320 kcal | Protein: 35g | Fat: 18g | Carbohydrates: 1g | Fiber: 0g | Sugar: 0g | Sodium: 200mg

Glycemic Index: Low (approximately 20)

Beef and Mushroom Stew

Prep Time: 10 minutes | Cook Time: 40 minutes | Serves: 2

Ingredients:

- 200 g/7 oz beef stew meat, cubed
- 150 g/5 oz mushrooms, sliced
- 1 small onion, chopped
- 2 garlic cloves, minced
- 1 carrot, sliced
- 1 celery stalk, chopped
- 400 ml beef broth (low-sodium)
- 1 tbsp olive oil
- 1 tsp dried thyme
- 1 bay leaf
- Salt and pepper, to taste
- Fresh parsley, chopped (optional, for garnish)

Instructions:

1. Heat olive oil in a large pot over medium heat. Add the beef and brown on all sides, about 5 minutes.
2. Add the onion, garlic, carrot, and celery. Sauté for 5 minutes until the vegetables are softened.
3. Stir in the mushrooms and cook for another 3-4 minutes.
4. Pour in the beef broth, and add thyme and bay leaf. Bring to a boil, then reduce heat, cover, and simmer for 30 minutes, until the beef is tender.
5. Remove bay leaf. Season with salt and pepper to taste. Garnish with fresh parsley if desired, and serve hot.

Nutritional Facts (Per Serving): Calories: 350 kcal | Protein: 28g | Fat: 18g | Carbohydrates: 15g | Fiber: 4g | Sugar: 5g | Sodium: 500mg

Glycemic Index: Low (approximately 40)

Grilled Lamb Chops with Mint Yogurt Sauce

Prep Time: 10 minutes | Cook Time: 15 minutes | Serves: 2

Ingredients:

- 4 lamb chops (approximately 150 g/5 oz each)
- 1 tbsp olive oil
- 1 tsp dried rosemary
- 1 tsp garlic powder
- Salt and pepper, to taste

Mint Yogurt Sauce:

- 100g Greek yogurt (unsweetened)
- 1 tbsp fresh mint, chopped
- 1 tsp lemon juice
- Salt and pepper, to taste

Instructions:

1. Preheat the grill to medium-high heat.
2. Rub the lamb chops with olive oil, rosemary, garlic powder, salt, and pepper.
3. Grill the lamb chops for 3-4 minutes per side, or until they reach your desired level of doneness.
4. While the lamb chops are grilling, prepare the mint yogurt sauce by combining Greek yogurt, chopped mint, lemon juice, salt, and pepper in a small bowl.
5. Serve the lamb chops hot, accompanied by the mint yogurt sauce.

Nutritional Facts (Per Serving): Calories: 450 kcal | Protein: 40g | Fat: 30g | Carbohydrates: 5g | Fiber: 1g | Sugar: 3g | Sodium: 250mg

Glycemic Index: Low (approximately 30)

CHAPTER 10: Satisfying Vegetarian Favorites

Stuffed Bell Peppers with Quinoa

Prep Time: 15 minutes | Cook Time: 30 minutes | Serves: 2

Ingredients:

- 2 large bell peppers, halved and seeds removed
- 100 g/3,3 oz quinoa, rinsed
- 200 ml vegetable broth (low-sodium)
- 1 small onion, chopped
- 1 garlic clove, minced
- 1 small zucchini, diced
- 50 g/2 oz cherry tomatoes, halved
- 1 tsp dried oregano
- 1 tbsp olive oil
- Salt and pepper, to taste
- 30g feta cheese, crumbled (optional)

Instructions:

1. Cook quinoa over medium heat for 15 minutes.
2. Sauté onion, garlic, and zucchini in olive oil until softened. Stir in quinoa, tomatoes, oregano, salt, and pepper. Mix well.
3. Stuff the bell pepper halves with the quinoa mixture and place in a baking dish.
4. Cover with foil and bake at 180°C (350°F) for 25-30 minutes until peppers are tender.
5. Sprinkle with feta cheese, if using, and serve.

Nutritional Facts (Per Serving): Calories: 280 kcal | Protein: 8g | Fat: 12g | Carbohydrates: 34g | Fiber: 7g | Sugar: 9g | Sodium: 300mg

Glycemic Index: Low (approximately 35)

Eggplant Parmesan

Prep Time: 15 minutes | Cook Time: 25 minutes | Serves: 2

Ingredients:

- 1 medium eggplant, sliced into rounds
- 200 g/5 oz marinara sauce (low-sodium)
- 50 g/2 oz Parmesan cheese, grated
- 50 g/2 oz mozzarella cheese, shredded
- 1/2 cup whole wheat breadcrumbs
- 1 egg, beaten
- 1 tbsp olive oil
- 1 tsp dried oregano
- Salt and pepper, to taste
- Fresh basil leaves for garnish (optional)

Instructions:

1. Preheat oven to 190°C (375°F).
2. Dip eggplant slices in beaten egg, coat with breadcrumbs, and place on a baking sheet. Drizzle with olive oil and bake for 20 minutes, turning once.
3. Layer eggplant slices with marinara sauce, Parmesan, and mozzarella. Repeat layers.
4. Sprinkle with oregano, salt, and pepper. Bake for 15 minutes until cheese is melted and bubbly.
5. Serve hot.

Nutritional Facts (Per Serving): Calories: 350 kcal | Protein: 15g | Fat: 20g | Carbohydrates: 30g | Fiber: 8g | Sugar: 10g | Sodium: 450mg

Glycemic Index: Low (approximately 45)

Chickpea and Spinach Curry

Prep Time: 10 minutes | Cook Time: 20 minutes | Serves: 2

Ingredients:

- 1 can (400 g/14 oz) chickpeas, drained and rinsed
- 100 g/3,3 oz fresh spinach leaves
- 1 small onion, chopped
- 2 garlic cloves, minced
- 1 tbsp olive oil
- 1 tsp ground cumin
- 1 tsp ground coriander
- 1/2 tsp ground turmeric
- 1/2 tsp ground ginger
- 200 g/7 oz canned diced tomatoes (no added salt)
- 100 ml coconut milk (light)
- Salt and pepper, to taste
- 1 tbsp fresh cilantro, chopped (for garnish)

Instructions:

1. Heat olive oil in a large pan over medium heat.
2. Add onion and garlic, sauté until softened, about 5 minutes.
3. Stir in cumin, coriander, turmeric, and ginger, cooking for 1 minute until fragrant.
4. Add chickpeas, diced tomatoes, and coconut milk. Simmer for 10 minutes until the sauce thickens.
5. Stir in spinach leaves and cook until wilted, about 2-3 minutes.

Nutritional Facts (Per Serving): Calories: 280 kcal | Protein: 10g | Fat: 12g | Carbohydrates: 34g | Fiber: 10g | Sugar: 8g | Sodium: 300mg

Glycemic Index: Low (approximately 35)

Grilled Tofu with Vegetables

Prep Time: 10 minutes | Cook Time: 15 minutes | Serves: 2

Ingredients:

- 200 g/7 oz firm tofu, sliced into rectangles
- 1 small zucchini, sliced
- 1 red bell pepper, sliced
- 1 small onion, sliced
- 1 tbsp olive oil
- 1 tbsp soy sauce (low-sodium)
- 1 tsp balsamic vinegar
- 1 tsp garlic powder
- Salt and pepper, to taste
- Fresh basil leaves for garnish (optional)

Instructions:

1. Preheat the grill to medium-high heat.
2. In a bowl, mix olive oil, soy sauce, balsamic vinegar, garlic powder, salt, and pepper. Marinate tofu slices in the mixture for at least 10 minutes.
3. Grill the tofu and vegetables for 3-4 minutes per side, until tofu is golden and vegetables are tender.
4. Serve hot, garnished with fresh basil leaves if desired.

Nutritional Facts (Per Serving): Calories: 240 kcal | Protein: 14g | Fat: 16g | Carbohydrates: 12g | Fiber: 4g | Sugar: 5g | Sodium: 400mg

Glycemic Index: Low (approximately 30)

Mushroom and Lentil Loaf

Prep Time: 15 minutes | Cook Time: 40 minutes | Serves: 2

Ingredients:

- 150 g/5 oz brown lentils, cooked
- 150 g/5 oz mushrooms, finely chopped
- 1 small onion, chopped
- 2 garlic cloves, minced
- 1 carrot, grated
- 1 celery stalk, chopped
- 1 tbsp olive oil
- 1 tbsp soy sauce (low-sodium)
- 1 tbsp tomato paste
- 1 tsp dried thyme
- 1/2 cup whole wheat breadcrumbs
- 1 egg, beaten
- Salt and pepper to taste

Instructions:

1. Preheat the oven to 180°C (350°F). Line a loaf pan with parchment paper.
2. Heat olive oil in a pan over medium heat. Sauté onion, garlic, carrot, celery, and mushrooms until softened, about 7-10 minutes.
3. In a large bowl, combine the cooked lentils, sautéed vegetables, soy sauce, tomato paste, thyme, breadcrumbs, and beaten egg. Mix well.
4. Season with salt and pepper, then press the mixture into the prepared loaf pan.
5. Bake for 30-40 minutes until firm and golden on top.
6. Let cool slightly before slicing and serving.

Nutritional Facts (Per Serving): Calories: 320 kcal | Protein: 14g | Fat: 10g | Carbohydrates: 40g | Fiber: 12g | Sugar: 7g | Sodium: 450mg

Glycemic Index: Low (approximately 35)

Cauliflower Steaks with Garlic Sauce

Prep Time: 10 minutes | Cook Time: 20 minutes | Serves: 2

Ingredients:

- 1 large cauliflower, cut into 2 thick steaks
- 2 tbsp olive oil
- 1 tsp paprika
- Salt and pepper, to taste

Garlic Sauce:

- 2 tbsp Greek yogurt (unsweetened)
- 1 garlic clove, minced
- 1 tbsp lemon juice
- 1 tbsp fresh parsley, chopped
- Salt and pepper, to taste

Instructions:

1. Preheat the oven to 200°C (400°F).
2. Brush both sides of the cauliflower steaks with olive oil and season with paprika, salt, and pepper.
3. Place the steaks on a baking sheet and roast for 15-20 minutes, flipping halfway, until tender and golden brown.
4. While the cauliflower is roasting, prepare the garlic sauce by mixing Greek yogurt, minced garlic, lemon juice, parsley, salt, and pepper in a small bowl.
5. Serve the cauliflower steaks hot, drizzled with the garlic sauce.

Nutritional Facts (Per Serving): Calories: 180 kcal | Protein: 4g | Fat: 14g | Carbohydrates: 10g | Fiber: 4g | Sugar: 3g | Sodium: 250mg

Glycemic Index: Low (approximately 30)

Zucchini Noodles with Pesto

Prep Time: 10 minutes | Cook Time: 5 minutes | Serves: 2

Ingredients:

- 2 medium zucchinis, spiralized into noodles
- 1/4 cup pesto sauce (store-bought or homemade)
- 1 tbsp olive oil
- 1 garlic clove, minced
- 2 tbsp Parmesan cheese, grated (optional)
- Salt and pepper, to taste
- Fresh basil leaves for garnish (optional)

Instructions:

1. Heat olive oil in a large skillet over medium heat. Add minced garlic and sauté for 1 minute until fragrant.
2. Add zucchini noodles to the skillet and cook for 2-3 minutes until just tender.
3. Remove from heat and toss the noodles with pesto sauce until evenly coated.
4. Season with salt and pepper to taste. Sprinkle with Parmesan cheese and garnish with fresh basil if desired. Serve immediately.

Nutritional Facts (Per Serving): Calories: 200 kcal | Protein: 4g | Fat: 18g | Carbohydrates: 8g | Fiber: 3g | Sugar: 5g | Sodium: 250mg

Glycemic Index: Low (approximately 30)

Veggie Stir-Fry with Cashews

Prep Time: 10 minutes | Cook Time: 10 minutes | Serves: 2

Ingredients:

- 1 small broccoli head, cut into florets
- 1 red bell pepper, sliced
- 1 small zucchini, sliced
- 1 carrot, julienned
- 2 garlic cloves, minced
- 1 tbsp olive oil
- 1 tbsp soy sauce (low-sodium)
- 1 tsp sesame oil
- 1/4 cup cashews, toasted
- Salt and pepper, to taste
- Fresh cilantro for garnish

Instructions:

1. Heat olive oil in a large skillet or wok over medium-high heat. Add garlic and sauté for 1 minute until fragrant.
2. Add broccoli, bell pepper, zucchini, and carrot. Stir-fry for 5-7 minutes until vegetables are tender-crisp.
3. Add soy sauce, sesame oil, salt, and pepper. Stir well to coat the vegetables.
4. Toss in toasted cashews and cook for an additional 1-2 minutes.
5. Garnish with fresh cilantro if desired and serve hot.

Nutritional Facts (Per Serving): Calories: 250 kcal | Protein: 6g | Fat: 18g | Carbohydrates: 18g | Fiber: 6g | Sugar: 7g | Sodium: 400mg

Glycemic Index: Low (approximately 30)

CHAPTER 11: Flavorful Seafood Delights

Shrimp and Avocado Salad

Prep Time: 10 minutes | Cook Time: 5 minutes | Serves: 2

Ingredients:

- 200 g/7 oz shrimp, peeled and deveined
- 1 large avocado, diced
- 1 small cucumber, diced
- 1/2 red onion, thinly sliced
- 1 tbsp olive oil
- 1 tbsp fresh lemon juice
- 1 tbsp fresh cilantro, chopped
- Salt and pepper, to taste

Instructions:

1. Heat a skillet over medium heat and add the shrimp. Cook for 2-3 minutes per side until pink and opaque. Remove from heat and let cool slightly.
2. In a large bowl, combine diced avocado, cucumber, red onion, and cooked shrimp.
3. Drizzle with olive oil and lemon juice, then toss gently to combine.
4. Season with salt and pepper to taste. Garnish with fresh cilantro and serve immediately.

Nutritional Facts (Per Serving): Calories: 300 kcal | Protein: 20g | Fat: 22g | Carbohydrates: 10g | Fiber: 6g | Sugar: 2g | Sodium: 400mg

Glycemic Index: Low (approximately 25)

Baked Tilapia with Lemon

Prep Time: 5 minutes | Cook Time: 15 minutes | Serves: 2

Ingredients:

- 2 tilapia fillets (about 150 g/5 oz each)
- 1 lemon, thinly sliced
- 1 tbsp olive oil
- 1 tsp garlic powder
- 1 tsp dried oregano
- Salt and pepper, to taste
- Fresh parsley, chopped (optional, for garnish)

Instructions:

1. Preheat the oven to 200°C (400°F). Line a baking sheet with parchment paper.
2. Place the tilapia fillets on the prepared baking sheet. Drizzle with olive oil and season with garlic powder, oregano, salt, and pepper.
3. Lay lemon slices over the tilapia fillets.
4. Bake for 12-15 minutes, or until the fish is opaque and flakes easily with a fork.
5. Garnish with fresh parsley if desired, and serve hot.

Nutritional Facts (Per Serving): Calories: 220 kcal | Protein: 28g | Fat: 10g | Carbohydrates: 4g | Fiber: 1g | Sugar: 0g | Sodium: 150mg

Glycemic Index: Low (approximately 20)

Grilled Scallops with Asparagus

Prep Time: 10 minutes | Cook Time: 10 minutes | Serves: 2

Ingredients:

- 200 g/7 oz scallops
- 200 g/7 oz asparagus, trimmed
- 1 tbsp olive oil
- 1 tbsp lemon juice
- 1 garlic clove, minced
- Salt and pepper, to taste
- Fresh parsley, chopped (optional, for garnish)

Instructions:

1. Preheat the grill to medium-high heat.
2. In a bowl, toss the scallops and asparagus with olive oil, lemon juice, minced garlic, salt, and pepper.
3. Grill the asparagus for 4-5 minutes, turning occasionally, until tender and slightly charred.
4. Grill the scallops for 2-3 minutes per side until they are opaque and have a slight char.
5. Serve the grilled scallops and asparagus hot, garnished with fresh parsley if desired.

Nutritional Facts (Per Serving): Calories: 250 kcal | Protein: 20g | Fat: 12g | Carbohydrates: 10g | Fiber: 4g | Sugar: 3g | Sodium: 320mg

Glycemic Index: Low (approximately 25)

Tuna Steak with Sesame Crust

Prep Time: 10 minutes | Cook Time: 6 minutes | Serves: 2

Ingredients:

- 2 tuna steaks (about 150 g/5 oz each)
- 2 tbsp sesame seeds (white or black, or a mix)
- 1 tbsp soy sauce (low-sodium)
- 1 tbsp olive oil
- 1 tsp sesame oil
- 1 garlic clove, minced
- 1 tsp fresh ginger, grated
- Salt and pepper, to taste
- Lemon wedges (optional, for serving)

Instructions:

1. In a small bowl, mix soy sauce, sesame oil, garlic, and ginger. Marinate the tuna steaks in the mixture for at least 10 minutes.
2. Press sesame seeds on both sides of each tuna steak to create a crust.
3. Heat olive oil in a skillet over medium-high heat.
4. Sear the tuna steaks for 2-3 minutes on each side for medium-rare, or longer if you prefer them more cooked.
5. Remove from heat and let rest for a minute. Serve with lemon wedges if desired.

Nutritional Facts (Per Serving): Calories: 300 kcal | Protein: 30g | Fat: 18g | Carbohydrates: 4g | Fiber: 1g | Sugar: 0g | Sodium: 250mg

Glycemic Index: Low (approximately 25)

Lobster Tails with Garlic Butter

Prep Time: 10 minutes | Cook Time: 12 minutes | Serves: 2

Ingredients:

- 2 lobster tails (about 150 g/5 oz each)
- 3 tbsp unsalted butter, melted
- 2 garlic cloves, minced
- 1 tbsp fresh lemon juice
- 1 tsp fresh parsley, chopped
- Salt and pepper, to taste
- Lemon wedges (optional, for serving)

Instructions:

1. Preheat the oven to 220°C (425°F) and prepare a baking sheet.
2. Using kitchen scissors, carefully cut through the top shell of each lobster tail, then gently pull the meat upward, leaving it attached at the base.
3. In a small bowl, mix melted butter, minced garlic, lemon juice, salt, and pepper.
4. Place the lobster tails on the baking sheet and brush generously with the garlic butter mixture.
5. Bake for 10-12 minutes, or until the lobster meat is opaque and slightly firm.
6. Garnish with fresh parsley and serve with lemon wedges if desired.

Nutritional Facts (Per Serving): Calories: 340 kcal | Protein: 28g | Fat: 24g | Carbohydrates: 2g | Fiber: 0g | Sugar: 0g | Sodium: 420mg

Glycemic Index: Low (approximately 20)

Crab Cakes with Spicy Aioli

Prep Time: 15 minutes | Cook Time: 10 minutes | Serves: 2

Ingredients:

- 200 g/7 oz lump crab meat
- 1/4 cup whole wheat breadcrumbs
- 1 egg, beaten
- 2 tbsp mayonnaise (low-fat)
- 1 tsp Dijon mustard
- 1 tsp lemon juice
- 1 tbsp fresh parsley, chopped
- 1 garlic clove, minced
- 1/2 tsp paprika
- Salt and pepper, to taste
- 2 tbsp olive oil (for frying)

Spicy Aioli:

- 2 tbsp mayonnaise (low-fat)
- 1 tsp sriracha or hot sauce
- 1 tsp lemon juice
- 1 garlic clove, minced

Instructions:

1. In a large bowl, combine crab meat, breadcrumbs, beaten egg, mayonnaise, Dijon mustard, lemon juice, parsley, minced garlic, paprika, salt, and pepper. Mix well.
2. Form the mixture into small patties.
3. Heat olive oil in a skillet over medium heat. Cook the crab cakes for 3-4 minutes on each side until golden brown and cooked through. Remove and let drain on paper towels.
4. For the spicy aioli, mix mayonnaise, sriracha, lemon juice, and garlic in a small bowl.
5. Serve the crab cakes hot with a side of spicy aioli.

Nutritional Facts (Per Serving): Calories: 320 kcal | Protein: 20g | Fat: 22g | Carbohydrates: 10g | Fiber: 1g | Sugar: 1g | Sodium: 450mg

Glycemic Index: Low (approximately 30)

Salmon with Dill Yogurt Sauce

Prep Time: 10 minutes | Cook Time: 15 minutes | Serves: 2

Ingredients:

- 2 salmon fillets (about 150 g/5 oz each)
- 1 tbsp olive oil
- 1 tsp lemon juice
- Salt and pepper, to taste

Dill Yogurt Sauce:

- 100 g/3,3 oz Greek yogurt (unsweetened)
- 1 tbsp fresh dill, chopped
- 1 tsp lemon juice
- 1 garlic clove, minced
- Salt and pepper, to taste

Instructions:

1. Preheat the oven to 200°C (400°F). Line a baking sheet with parchment paper.
2. Brush the salmon fillets with olive oil and lemon juice. Season with salt and pepper.
3. Place the salmon on the prepared baking sheet and bake for 12-15 minutes, or until the salmon is cooked through and flakes easily with a fork.
4. While the salmon is baking, prepare the dill yogurt sauce by mixing Greek yogurt, chopped dill, lemon juice, minced garlic, salt, and pepper in a small bowl.
5. Serve the salmon hot with a generous spoonful of dill yogurt sauce on top.

Nutritional Facts (Per Serving): Calories: 320 kcal | Protein: 28g | Fat: 20g | Carbohydrates: 3g | Fiber: 0g | Sugar: 1g | Sodium: 250mg

Glycemic Index: Low (approximately 25)

Cod with Tomato and Olive Sauce

Prep Time: 10 minutes | Cook Time: 15 minutes | Serves: 2

Ingredients:

- 2 cod fillets (about 150 g/5 oz each)
- 1 tbsp olive oil
- 1 small onion, chopped
- 2 garlic cloves, minced
- 200 g/7 oz canned diced tomatoes (no added salt)
- 50 g/2 oz Kalamata olives, pitted and sliced
- 1 tsp dried oregano
- Salt and pepper, to taste
- Fresh parsley, chopped (optional, for garnish)

Instructions:

1. Heat olive oil in a large skillet over medium heat. Add the chopped onion and sauté for 3-4 minutes until softened. Add the minced garlic and cook for another minute.
2. Stir in the diced tomatoes, olives, and oregano. Season with salt and pepper. Simmer the sauce for 5-7 minutes until slightly thickened.
3. Season the cod fillets with salt and pepper, then place them in the skillet with the tomato and olive sauce. Spoon some of the sauce over the fish.
4. Cover and cook for 6-8 minutes, or until the cod is opaque and flakes easily with a fork.
5. Garnish with fresh parsley if desired, and serve hot.

Nutritional Facts (Per Serving): Calories: 280 kcal | Protein: 30g | Fat: 12g | Carbohydrates: 8g | Fiber: 2g | Sugar: 3g | Sodium: 450mg

Glycemic Index: Low (approximately 30)

CHAPTER 12: Healthy Side Dishes

Roasted Brussels Sprouts with Balsamic Glaze

Prep Time: 10 minutes | Cook Time: 25 minutes | Serves: 2

Ingredients:

- 300 g/10 oz Brussels sprouts, trimmed and halved
- 2 tbsp balsamic vinegar
- 1 tbsp olive oil
- Salt and pepper, to taste
- 1 tsp honey or stevia (optional)

Instructions:

1. Preheat the oven to 200°C (400°F). Line a baking sheet with parchment paper.
2. Toss the Brussels sprouts with olive oil, salt, and pepper. Spread them out in a single layer on the baking sheet.
3. Roast for 25 minutes, stirring halfway through.
4. In a small saucepan, simmer balsamic vinegar and honey (if using) until it reduces by half, about 5 minutes.
5. Drizzle the balsamic glaze over the roasted Brussels sprouts and serve.

Nutritional Facts (Per Serving): Calories: 150 kcal | Protein: 4g | Fat: 8g | Carbohydrates: 18g | Fiber: 6g | Sugar: 7g | Sodium: 50mg

Glycemic Index: Low (approximately 30)

Steamed Broccoli with Lemon

Prep Time: 5 minutes | Cook Time: 5 minutes | Serves: 2

Ingredients:

- 300 g/10 oz broccoli florets
- 1 tbsp olive oil
- 1 tbsp fresh lemon juice
- Salt and pepper, to taste
- Lemon zest, for garnish (optional)

Instructions:

1. Steam the broccoli florets in a steamer basket over boiling water for 4-5 minutes, until tender-crisp.
2. Transfer the steamed broccoli to a bowl. Drizzle with olive oil and lemon juice.
3. Season with salt and pepper to taste. Garnish with lemon zest if desired, and serve.

Nutritional Facts (Per Serving): Calories: 100 kcal | Protein: 3g | Fat: 7g | Carbohydrates: 8g | Fiber: 4g | Sugar: 2g | Sodium: 50mg

Glycemic Index: Low (approximately 15)

Quinoa Pilaf with Herbs

Prep Time: 5 minutes | Cook Time: 15 minutes | Serves: 2

Ingredients:

- 100 g/3,3 oz quinoa, rinsed
- 200 ml vegetable broth (low-sodium)
- 1 tbsp olive oil
- 1 small onion, chopped
- 1 garlic clove, minced
- 1 tsp dried thyme
- 1 tbsp fresh parsley, chopped
- Salt and pepper, to taste

Instructions:

1. Heat olive oil in a pot over medium heat. Sauté the onion and garlic until softened, about 3 minutes.
2. Add the rinsed quinoa, vegetable broth, and dried thyme. Bring to a boil, then reduce heat, cover, and simmer for 15 minutes, or until the quinoa is cooked, and the liquid is absorbed.
3. Fluff the quinoa with a fork, stir in fresh parsley, and season with salt and pepper to taste. Serve hot.

Nutritional Facts (Per Serving): Calories: 180 kcal | Protein: 6g | Fat: 7g | Carbohydrates: 24g | Fiber: 3g | Sugar: 2g | Sodium: 150mg

Glycemic Index: Low (approximately 35)

Garlic Mashed Cauliflower

Prep Time: 5 minutes | Cook Time: 10 minutes | Serves: 2

Ingredients:

- 1 medium head of cauliflower, chopped into florets
- 2 tbsp Greek yogurt (unsweetened)
- 2 garlic cloves, minced
- 1 tbsp olive oil
- Salt and pepper, to taste
- Fresh parsley, chopped (optional, for garnish)

Instructions:

1. Steam the cauliflower florets in a steamer basket over boiling water for 8-10 minutes until tender.
2. Transfer the steamed cauliflower to a food processor. Add the minced garlic, Greek yogurt, olive oil, salt, and pepper. Blend until smooth and creamy.
3. Adjust seasoning if needed. Garnish with fresh parsley if desired, and serve hot.

Nutritional Facts (Per Serving): Calories: 120 kcal | Protein: 4g | Fat: 8g | Carbohydrates: 10g | Fiber: 4g | Sugar: 3g | Sodium: 100mg

Glycemic Index: Low (approximately 15)

Sautéed Spinach with Pine Nuts

Prep Time: 5 minutes | Cook Time: 5 minutes | Serves: 2

Ingredients:

- 200 g/7 oz fresh spinach leaves
- 2 tbsp pine nuts
- 1 tbsp olive oil
- 2 garlic cloves, minced
- Salt and pepper, to taste
- Lemon zest, for garnish (optional)

Instructions:

1. Heat a large skillet over medium heat. Add the pine nuts and toast for 2-3 minutes, stirring frequently until golden. Remove and set aside.
2. In the same skillet, heat olive oil. Add minced garlic and sauté for 1 minute until fragrant.
3. Add the spinach leaves and cook, stirring constantly, for 2-3 minutes until wilted.
4. Season with salt and pepper. Sprinkle with toasted pine nuts and garnish with lemon zest if desired. Serve immediately.

Nutritional Facts (Per Serving): Calories: 150 kcal | Protein: 4g | Fat: 12g | Carbohydrates: 6g | Fiber: 3g | Sugar: 1g | Sodium: 100mg

Glycemic Index: Low (approximately 15)

Brown Rice with Mushrooms

Prep Time: 5 minutes | Cook Time: 30 minutes | Serves: 2

Ingredients:

- 100 g/3,3 oz brown rice
- 200 g/7 oz mushrooms, sliced
- 1 small onion, chopped
- 2 garlic cloves, minced
- 1 tbsp olive oil
- 300 ml vegetable broth (low-sodium)
- 1 tsp dried thyme
- Salt and pepper, to taste
- Fresh parsley, chopped (optional, for garnish)

Instructions:

1. Rinse the brown rice under cold water. In a medium pot, bring the vegetable broth to a boil. Add the rice, reduce heat, cover, and simmer for 25-30 minutes, or until the rice is tender and the liquid is absorbed.
2. While the rice is cooking, heat olive oil in a large skillet over medium heat. Add the chopped onion and sauté for 3 minutes until softened.
3. Add the garlic and mushrooms to the skillet, and cook for 5-7 minutes until the mushrooms are golden and tender.
4. Stir in the cooked rice and thyme. Season with salt and pepper to taste.
5. Garnish with fresh parsley if desired, and serve hot

Nutritional Facts (Per Serving): Calories: 250 kcal | Protein: 6g | Fat: 9g | Carbohydrates: 38g | Fiber: 4g | Sugar: 3g | Sodium: 150mg

Glycemic Index: Medium (approximately 50)

Roasted Sweet Potatoes

Prep Time: 5 minutes | Cook Time: 25 minutes | Serves: 2

Ingredients:

- 2 medium sweet potatoes, peeled and cubed
- 1 tbsp olive oil
- 1 tsp ground cinnamon (optional)
- Salt and pepper, to taste

Instructions:

1. Preheat the oven to 200°C (400°F). Line a baking sheet with parchment paper.
2. In a large bowl, toss the sweet potato cubes with olive oil, cinnamon (if using), salt, and pepper.
3. Spread the sweet potatoes in a single layer on the prepared baking sheet.
4. Roast for 25-30 minutes, stirring halfway through, until the sweet potatoes are tender and golden brown.
5. Serve hot.

Nutritional Facts (Per Serving): Calories: 180 kcal | Protein: 2g | Fat: 7g | Carbohydrates: 30g | Fiber: 5g | Sugar: 7g | Sodium: 150mg

Glycemic Index: Medium (approximately 60)

Cauliflower Rice with Cilantro

Prep Time: 5 minutes | Cook Time: 5 minutes | Serves: 2

Ingredients:

- 1 medium head of cauliflower, grated or pulsed into rice-sized pieces
- 1 tbsp olive oil
- 2 garlic cloves, minced
- 1 tbsp fresh cilantro, chopped
- Salt and pepper, to taste
- 1 tbsp lime juice (optional, for extra flavor)

Instructions:

1. Finely chop the cauliflower or place it in a food processor and pulse until it resembles grains of rice. Be careful not to over-process, as it can become mushy.
2. Heat olive oil in a large skillet over medium heat. Add the minced garlic and sauté for 1 minute until fragrant.
3. Add the cauliflower rice to the skillet and cook, stirring frequently, for 3-5 minutes until tender.
4. Stir in the chopped cilantro and season with salt and pepper. Add lime juice if desired.
5. Serve hot.

Nutritional Facts (Per Serving): Calories: 100 kcal | Protein: 3g | Fat: 7g | Carbohydrates: 8g | Fiber: 4g | Sugar: 3g | Sodium: 100mg

Glycemic Index: Low (approximately 15)

CHAPTER 13: Savory Snack Ideas

Roasted Chickpeas with Spices

Prep Time: 5 minutes | Cook Time: 30 minutes | Serves: 2

Ingredients:

- 1 can (400 g/14 oz) chickpeas, drained and rinsed
- 1 tbsp olive oil
- 1 tsp smoked paprika
- 1/2 tsp ground cumin
- 1/2 tsp garlic powder
- 1/4 tsp cayenne pepper (optional, for heat)
- Salt and pepper, to taste

Instructions:

1. Preheat the oven to 200°C (400°F). Line a baking sheet with parchment paper.
2. Pat the chickpeas dry with a paper towel to remove excess moisture.
3. Toss chickpeas with olive oil, spices, salt, and pepper.
4. Spread the chickpeas in a single layer on the prepared baking sheet.
5. Roast for 25-30 minutes, shaking the pan halfway through, until the chickpeas are crispy and golden brown.
6. Let cool slightly before serving.

Nutritional Facts (Per Serving): Calories: 150 kcal | Protein: 6g | Fat: 6g | Carbohydrates: 19g | Fiber: 5g | Sugar: 1g | Sodium: 240mg

Glycemic Index: Low (approximately 30)

Baked Zucchini Chips

Prep Time: 10 minutes | Cook Time: 20 minutes | Serves: 2

Ingredients:

- 1 large zucchini, thinly sliced
- 1 tbsp olive oil
- 1/2 tsp garlic powder
- 1/2 tsp paprika
- Salt and pepper, to taste

Instructions:

1. Preheat the oven to 200°C (400°F). Line a baking sheet with parchment paper.
2. Toss zucchini slices with olive oil, garlic powder, paprika, salt, and pepper until evenly coated.
3. Arrange the slices in a single layer on the prepared baking sheet.
4. Bake for 15-20 minutes, or until the chips are golden and crispy, flipping them halfway through.
5. Let cool slightly before serving.

Nutritional Facts (Per Serving): Calories: 100 kcal | Protein: 2g | Fat: 7g | Carbohydrates: 8g | Fiber: 2g | Sugar: 3g | Sodium: 150mg

Glycemic Index: Low (approximately 15)

Almond and Seed Crackers

Prep Time: 10 minutes | Cook Time: 15 minutes | Serves: 2

Ingredients:

- 1 cup almond flour
- 2 tbsp mixed seeds (e.g., chia, sesame, flax)
- 1 tbsp olive oil
- 1 egg, beaten
- 1/2 tsp garlic powder
- 1/2 tsp salt
- 1/4 tsp black pepper

Instructions:

1. Preheat the oven to 180°C (350°F). Line a baking sheet with parchment paper.
2. In a bowl, mix almond flour, seeds, garlic powder, salt, and pepper. Add the beaten egg and olive oil, stirring until a dough forms.
3. Place the dough between two sheets of parchment paper and roll out to about 1/8-inch thickness.
4. Remove the top sheet of parchment paper and cut the dough into cracker shapes.
5. Transfer the parchment paper with the cut dough onto the baking sheet. Bake for 12-15 minutes until golden and crisp.
6. Let cool before serving.

Nutritional Facts (Per Serving): Calories: 200 kcal | Protein: 7g | Fat: 16g | Carbohydrates: 6g | Fiber: 3g | Sugar: 1g | Sodium: 200mg

Glycemic Index: Low (approximately 15)

Deviled Eggs with Avocado

Prep Time: 10 minutes | Cook Time: 10 minutes | Serves: 2

Ingredients:

- 4 large eggs
- 1 ripe avocado
- 1 tsp lime juice
- 1/2 tsp garlic powder
- 1 tbsp Greek yogurt (unsweetened)
- Salt and pepper, to taste
- Paprika, for garnish (optional)

Instructions:

1. Place the eggs in a saucepan and cover with water. Bring to a boil, then reduce the heat and simmer for 9-10 minutes. Transfer the eggs to an ice bath to cool, then peel and halve them.
2. Scoop out the yolks and place them in a bowl. Add the avocado, lime juice, Greek yogurt, garlic powder, salt, and pepper. Mash until smooth.
3. Spoon or pipe the avocado mixture back into the egg whites.
4. Garnish with paprika if desired, and serve.

Nutritional Facts (Per Serving): Calories: 200 kcal | Protein: 10g | Fat: 16g | Carbohydrates: 5g | Fiber: 3g | Sugar: 1g | Sodium: 150mg

Glycemic Index: Low (approximately 20)

Spicy Pumpkin Seeds

Prep Time: 5 minutes | Cook Time: 20 minutes | Serves: 2

Ingredients:

- 1 cup raw pumpkin seeds
- 1 tbsp olive oil
- 1 tsp smoked paprika
- 1/2 tsp cayenne pepper (adjust to taste)
- 1/2 tsp garlic powder
- Salt, to taste

Instructions:

1. Preheat the oven to 180°C (350°F). Line a baking sheet with parchment paper.
2. In a bowl, toss the pumpkin seeds with olive oil, smoked paprika, cayenne pepper, garlic powder, and salt until evenly coated.
3. Spread the seeds in a single layer on the prepared baking sheet.
4. Bake for 15-20 minutes, stirring halfway through, until the seeds are golden and crispy.
5. Let cool slightly before serving.

Nutritional Facts (Per Serving): Calories: 180 kcal | Protein: 8g | Fat: 14g | Carbohydrates: 5g | Fiber: 2g | Sugar: 0g | Sodium: 150mg

Glycemic Index: Low (approximately 15)

Cheese and Olive Skewers

Prep Time: 5 minutes | No Cook | Serves: 2

Ingredients:

- 100 g/3,3 oz cheese (such as cheddar or mozzarella), cubed
- 12 pitted olives (green or black)
- 1 tbsp fresh basil leaves (optional)
- 1 tbsp balsamic glaze (optional, for drizzling)

Instructions:

1. Thread a cube of cheese, an olive, and a basil leaf (if using) onto small skewers or toothpicks.
2. Repeat until all ingredients are used.
3. Arrange the skewers on a serving plate.
4. Drizzle with balsamic glaze if desired, and serve.

Nutritional Facts (Per Serving): Calories: 250 kcal | Protein: 12g | Fat: 20g | Carbohydrates: 2g | Fiber: 0g | Sugar: 0g | Sodium: 450mg

Glycemic Index: Low (approximately 15)

Veggie Sticks with Hummus

Prep Time: 15 minutes | Cook Time: No Cook | Serves: 2

Ingredients:

- 1 can (400 g/14 oz) chickpeas, drained and rinsed
- 2 tbsp tahini
- 2 tbsp lemon juice
- 1 garlic clove, minced
- 2 tbsp olive oil
- 1/2 tsp ground cumin
- Salt, to taste
- 2-3 tbsp water (as needed for consistency)
- 1 medium carrot, cut into sticks
- 1 cucumber, cut into sticks
- 1 red bell pepper, sliced
- 1 tbsp olive oil (optional, for drizzling)
- 1 tsp paprika (optional, for garnish)

Instructions:

1. In a food processor, combine chickpeas, tahini, lemon juice, garlic, olive oil, cumin, and salt. Blend until smooth, adding water as needed to reach your desired consistency.
2. Arrange the carrot sticks, cucumber sticks, and red bell pepper slices on a serving plate.
3. Place the homemade hummus in a small bowl, drizzle with olive oil, and sprinkle with paprika if desired. Serve the veggie sticks with the hummus for dipping.

Nutritional Facts (Per Serving): Calories: 240 kcal | Protein: 8g | Fat: 14g | Carbohydrates: 22g | Fiber: 7g | Sugar: 7g | Sodium: 240mg

Glycemic Index: Low (approximately 30)

Kale Chips with Parmesan

Prep Time: 5 minutes | Cook Time: 15 minutes | Serves: 2

Ingredients:

- 100 g/3,3 oz kale leaves, stems removed and torn into bite-sized pieces
- 1 tbsp olive oil
- 2 tbsp grated Parmesan cheese
- 1/2 tsp garlic powder
- Salt, to taste

Instructions:

1. Preheat the oven to 150°C (300°F). Line a baking sheet with parchment paper.
2. In a large bowl, toss the kale leaves with olive oil, garlic powder, and salt until evenly coated.
3. Spread the kale in a single layer on the prepared baking sheet.
4. Bake for 10 minutes, then sprinkle with grated Parmesan. Bake for an additional 5 minutes until the kale is crispy and the Parmesan is melted.
5. Let cool slightly before serving.

Nutritional Facts (Per Serving): Calories: 100 kcal | Protein: 4g | Fat: 8g | Carbohydrates: 5g | Fiber: 2g | Sugar: 1g | Sodium: 150mg

Glycemic Index: Low (approximately 15)

CHAPTER 14: Sweet Treats without the Guilt

Frozen Yogurt Bark with Berries

Prep Time: 10 minutes | No Cook (Freezing Time: 2 hours) | Serves: 2

Ingredients:

- 200 g/7 oz Greek yogurt (unsweetened)
- 1 tbsp honey or a sugar-free sweetener (optional)
- 50 g/2 oz mixed berries
- 1 tbsp chopped nuts (e.g., almonds, walnuts) (optional)
- 1 tsp chia seeds (optional)

Instructions:

1. In a bowl, mix the Greek yogurt with honey or a sugar-free sweetener, if using.
2. Line a baking sheet with parchment paper and spread the yogurt mixture evenly across it, about 1/4-inch thick.
3. Top with berries, nuts, and chia seeds.
4. Place the baking sheet in the freezer and freeze for at least 2 hours, or until the yogurt is firm.
5. Once frozen, break the yogurt bark into pieces and serve immediately or store in an airtight container in the freezer.

Nutritional Facts (Per Serving): Calories: 120 kcal | Protein: 8g | Fat: 4g | Carbohydrates: 12g | Fiber: 3g | Sugar: 8g | Sodium: 40mg

Glycemic Index: Low (approximately 30)

Chia Seed Pudding with Coconut

Prep Time: 5 minutes | No Cook (Chill Time: 4 hours or overnight) | Serves: 2

Ingredients:

- 2 tbsp chia seeds
- 200 ml unsweetened coconut milk
- 1 tbsp shredded coconut (unsweetened)
- 1 tsp vanilla extract
- 1 tbsp honey or sugar-free sweetener (optional)
- Fresh berries or sliced almonds for topping (optional)

Instructions:

1. In a bowl, mix chia seeds, coconut milk, shredded coconut, vanilla extract, and honey or sweetener, if using.
2. Stir well and let sit for 5 minutes, then stir again to prevent clumping.
3. Cover and refrigerate for at least 4 hours or overnight until the pudding thickens.
4. Serve chilled, topped with fresh berries or sliced almonds if desired.

Nutritional Facts (Per Serving): Calories: 150 kcal | Protein: 3g | Fat: 10g | Carbohydrates: 12g | Fiber: 6g | Sugar: 3g | Sodium: 60mg

Glycemic Index: Low (approximately 30)

Chocolate-Covered Almond and Berry Truffles

Prep Time: 15 minutes | No Cook (Chill Time: 30 minutes) | Serves: 2

Ingredients:

- 100 g/3,3 oz fresh or frozen raspberries (or other low GI berries like blueberries)
- 50 g/2 oz almonds, finely chopped
- 1 tsp almond butter (or other nut butter)
- 100 g/3,3 oz dark chocolate (70% cacao or higher), chopped
- 1 tsp coconut oil (optional, for easier melting)
- 1/2 tsp sea salt (optional, for garnish)

Instructions:

1. Mash the raspberries in a bowl until they form a thick paste. Add chopped almonds and almond butter, mixing until well combined.
2. Roll the mixture into small truffle-sized balls and place them on a parchment-lined baking sheet. Freeze for about 15 minutes to firm up.
3. Melt the dark chocolate and coconut oil (if using) in a double boiler or microwave in 30-second intervals, stirring until smooth.
4. Dip each berry-almond truffle into the melted chocolate, coating them evenly. Place them back on the parchment paper.
5. Sprinkle with sea salt if desired and refrigerate for about 30 minutes until the chocolate is set.
6. Serve chilled or at room temperature.

Nutritional Facts (Per Serving): Calories: 180 kcal | Protein: 4g | Fat: 14g | Carbohydrates: 12g | Fiber: 5g | Sugar: 5g | Sodium: 50mg

Glycemic Index: Low (approximately 25)

Stuffed Apple Rings with Peanut Butter and Granola

Prep Time: 10 minutes | No Cook | Serves: 2

Ingredients:

- 1 large apple, cored and sliced into rings
- 2 tbsp natural peanut butter (unsweetened)
- 2 tbsp granola (sugar-free)
- 1 tbsp chopped nuts (e.g., almonds, walnuts)
- 1 tbsp dried cranberries or raisins
- 1/2 tsp cinnamon
- 1 tbsp honey or maple syrup (optional, for drizzling)

Instructions:

1. Slice the apple into thick rings and remove the core from each slice.
2. Spread a layer of peanut butter on each apple ring.
3. Sprinkle granola, chopped nuts, and dried cranberries or raisins over the peanut butter.
4. Lightly dust with cinnamon for added flavor.
5. Drizzle honey or maple syrup over the top if desired.
6. Serve immediately, or refrigerate for a cool, refreshing snack.

Nutritional Facts (Per Serving): Calories: 250 kcal | Protein: 6g | Fat: 12g | Carbohydrates: 30g | Fiber: 6g | Sugar: 16g | Sodium: 60mg

Glycemic Index: Low (approximately 35)

Greek Yogurt Popsicles with Berries

Prep Time: 10 minutes | No Cook (Freezing Time: 4 hours) | Serves: 2

Ingredients:

- 200 g/7 oz Greek yogurt (unsweetened)
- 1/4 cup mixed berries (e.g., strawberries, blueberries, raspberries)
- 1 tbsp honey or sugar-free sweetener (optional)
- 1 tsp vanilla extract (optional)

Instructions:

1. In a bowl, mix Greek yogurt with honey or sweetener and vanilla extract, if using.
2. Gently fold in the mixed berries.
3. Spoon the mixture into popsicle molds.
4. Insert sticks and freeze for at least 4 hours, or until fully set.
5. To serve, run the molds under warm water to release the popsicles.

Nutritional Facts (Per Serving): Calories: 100 kcal | Protein: 6g | Fat: 2g | Carbohydrates: 12g | Fiber: 2g | Sugar: 8g | Sodium: 40mg

Glycemic Index: Low (approximately 30)

Cinnamon-Spiced Nuts

Prep Time: 5 minutes | Cook Time: 10 minutes | Serves: 2

Ingredients:

- 1 cup mixed nuts (e.g., almonds, walnuts, pecans)
- 1 tbsp melted coconut oil
- 1 tsp ground cinnamon
- 1/2 tsp vanilla extract
- 1 tbsp stevia or erythritol (optional, for sweetness)
- Pinch of salt

Instructions:

1. Preheat the oven to 180°C (350°F). Line a baking sheet with parchment paper.
2. In a bowl, toss the mixed nuts with melted coconut oil, cinnamon, vanilla extract, stevia or erythritol (if using), and a pinch of salt until evenly coated.
3. Spread the nuts in a single layer on the prepared baking sheet.
4. Bake for 8-10 minutes, stirring halfway through, until the nuts are toasted and fragrant.
5. Let cool before serving or storing in an airtight container.

Nutritional Facts (Per Serving): Calories: 220 kcal | Protein: 6g | Fat: 20g | Carbohydrates: 6g | Fiber: 3g | Sugar: 1g | Sodium: 50mg

Glycemic Index: Low (approximately 20)

Banana Oat Cookies

Prep Time: 5 minutes | Cook Time: 15 minutes | Serves: 2

Ingredients:

- 1 ripe banana, mashed
- 1/2 cup rolled oats (gluten-free if needed)
- 1 tbsp almond butter or peanut butter (unsweetened)
- 1/2 tsp cinnamon
- 1/4 tsp vanilla extract
- 1 tbsp chopped nuts (optional)
- 1 tbsp dark chocolate chips (optional, sugar-free)

Instructions:

1. Preheat the oven to 180°C (350°F). Line a baking sheet with parchment paper.
2. In a bowl, mix the mashed banana, oats, almond butter, cinnamon, and vanilla extract until well combined.
3. Fold in the chopped nuts and dark chocolate chips if using.
4. Drop spoonfuls of the mixture onto the prepared baking sheet, flattening slightly with the back of a spoon.
5. Bake for 12-15 minutes, or until the edges are golden, and the cookies are set.
6. Let cool on a wire rack before serving.

Nutritional Facts (Per Serving): Calories: 160 kcal | Protein: 4g | Fat: 6g | Carbohydrates: 24g | Fiber: 4g | Sugar: 8g | Sodium: 50mg

Glycemic Index: Low (approximately 40)

Low-Sugar Granola Bars

Prep Time: 10 minutes | Cook Time: 20 minutes | Serves: 2

Ingredients:

- 1 cup rolled oats
- 1/4 cup almond flour
- 2 tbsp flaxseeds
- 1/4 cup unsweetened almond butter or peanut butter
- 1/4 cup unsweetened applesauce
- 1 tsp vanilla extract
- 2 tbsp sugar-free maple syrup or honey
- 1/2 tsp ground cinnamon
- 1/4 cup chopped nuts (e.g., almonds, walnuts)
- 1/4 cup unsweetened dried fruit (e.g., cranberries, raisins) or dark chocolate chips (optional)

Instructions:

1. Preheat the oven to 180°C (350°F). Line a 8x8-inch baking pan with parchment paper.
2. Mix all ingredients in a bowl until well combined.
3. Press the mixture firmly into the prepared baking pan.
4. Bake for 18-20 minutes, or until the edges are golden, and the center is set.
5. Let cool completely in the pan before lifting out and cutting into bars.

Nutritional Facts (Per Serving): Calories: 200 kcal | Protein: 5g | Fat: 12g | Carbohydrates: 18g | Fiber: 4g | Sugar: 4g | Sodium: 50mg

Glycemic Index: Low (approximately 30)

CHAPTER 15: Low-Sugar Baking Delights

Sugar-Free Banana Bread

Prep Time: 10 minutes | Cook Time: 50 minutes | Serves: 2

Ingredients:

- 2 ripe bananas, mashed
- 1 cup almond flour
- 1/4 cup coconut flour
- 2 eggs
- 1/4 cup unsweetened almond milk
- 1/4 cup melted coconut oil
- 1 tsp vanilla extract
- 1 tsp baking soda
- 1/2 tsp baking powder
- 1/2 tsp cinnamon
- 1/4 tsp salt
- 1/4 cup chopped nuts or sugar-free dark chocolate chips (optional)

Instructions:

1. Preheat oven to 180°C (350°F). Grease or line a small loaf pan.
2. Mix bananas, eggs, almond milk, coconut oil, and vanilla in a bowl.
3. Add almond flour, coconut flour, baking soda, and cinnamon. Stir to combine.
4. Fold in nuts or chocolate chips if using.
5. Pour batter into the pan and bake for 45-50 minutes, until a toothpick comes out clean.
6. Cool in the pan for 10 minutes, then transfer to a rack to cool completely.

Nutritional Facts (Per Serving): Calories: 180 kcal | Protein: 6g | Fat: 12g | Carbohydrates: 15g | Fiber: 4g | Sugar: 5g | Sodium: 150mg

Glycemic Index: Low (approximately 35)

Blueberry Scones

Prep Time: 10 minutes | Cook Time: 20 minutes | Serves: 2

Ingredients:

- 1 cup almond flour
- 1/4 cup coconut flour
- 1/4 tsp baking soda
- 1/4 tsp salt
- 2 tbsp cold unsalted butter, cubed
- 1 egg
- 2 tbsp unsweetened almond milk
- 1 tsp vanilla extract
- 1/4 cup fresh or frozen blueberries
- 1-2 tbsp stevia (optional)

Instructions:

1. Preheat oven to 180°C (350°F). Line a baking sheet with parchment paper.
2. Mix flours, baking soda, and salt. Cut in butter until crumbly.
3. Whisk egg, almond milk, vanilla, and sweetener (if using) in a separate bowl.
4. Combine the wet and dry ingredients, then gently fold in the blueberries.
5. Drop spoonfuls of the dough onto the prepared baking sheet, forming small scones.
6. Bake for 18-20 minutes until golden brown. Cool slightly before serving.

Nutritional Facts (Per Serving): Calories: 200 kcal | Protein: 6g | Fat: 16g | Carbohydrates: 10g | Fiber: 4g | Sugar: 3g | Sodium: 150mg

Glycemic Index: Low (approximately 30)

Carrot Cake
with Cream Cheese Frosting

Prep Time: 15 minutes | Cook Time: 25 minutes | Serves: 2

Ingredients:

- 1 cup almond flour
- 1/4 cup coconut flour
- 1/2 tsp baking soda
- 1/2 tsp cinnamon
- 1/4 tsp nutmeg
- 1/4 tsp salt
- 2 eggs
- 1/4 cup melted coconut oil
- 1/4 cup unsweetened applesauce
- 1/4 cup finely grated carrots
- 1-2 tbsp stevia or erythritol (optional)
- 100 g/3,3 oz cream cheese (low-fat, softened)
- 1-2 tbsp stevia or erythritol (optional)
- 1 tsp vanilla extract

Instructions:

1. Preheat oven to 180°C (350°F). Line a small cake pan.
2. Mix flours, baking soda, spices, and salt. In another bowl, whisk eggs, coconut oil, applesauce, and sweetener. Combine with dry ingredients, then fold in carrots.
3. Pour batter into the pan and bake for 20-25 minutes. Let the cake cool completely.
4. Beat cream cheese, sweetener, and vanilla until smooth.
5. Spread over cooled cake and serve.

Nutritional Facts (Per Serving): Calories: 250 kcal | Protein: 7g | Fat: 20g | Carbohydrates: 10g | Fiber: 4g | Sugar: 5g | Sodium: 200mg

Glycemic Index: Low (approximately 30)

Oatmeal Cookies
with Dark Chocolate

Prep Time: 10 minutes | Cook Time: 15 minutes | Serves: 2

Ingredients:

- 1 cup rolled oats (gluten-free if needed)
- 1/4 cup almond flour
- 1/4 tsp baking soda
- 1/4 tsp salt
- 1 egg
- 1/4 cup coconut oil, melted
- 1 tsp vanilla extract
- 1-2 tbsp stevia or erythritol (optional)
- 1/4 cup dark chocolate chips (sugar-free)

Instructions:

1. Preheat the oven to 180°C (350°F). Line a baking sheet with parchment paper.
2. In a bowl, mix oats, almond flour, baking soda, and salt.
3. In another bowl, whisk together melted coconut oil, egg, vanilla extract, and sweetener (if using).
4. Combine wet and dry ingredients, then fold in dark chocolate chips.
5. Drop spoonfuls of the dough onto the prepared baking sheet.
6. Bake for 12-15 minutes until the edges are golden. Let cool before serving.

Nutritional Facts (Per Serving): Calories: 180 kcal | Protein: 4g | Fat: 12g | Carbohydrates: 14g | Fiber: 3g | Sugar: 4g | Sodium: 120mg

Glycemic Index: Low (approximately 35)

Almond Flour Blueberry Muffins

Prep Time: 10 minutes | Cook Time: 20 minutes | Serves: 2

Ingredients:

- 1 cup almond flour
- 1/4 tsp baking soda
- 1/4 tsp salt
- 1 large egg
- 2 tbsp unsweetened almond milk
- 2 tbsp melted coconut oil
- 1 tsp vanilla extract
- 1/4 cup fresh or frozen blueberries
- 1-2 tbsp stevia or erythritol (optional, for sweetness)

Instructions:

1. Preheat the oven to 180°C (350°F). Line a muffin tin with 4 paper liners.
2. In a bowl, mix almond flour, baking soda, and salt.
3. In another bowl, whisk together the egg, almond milk, melted coconut oil, vanilla extract, and stevia or erythritol (if using).
4. Combine the wet and dry ingredients, then gently fold in the blueberries.
5. Divide the batter evenly among the 4 muffin liners.
6. Bake for 18-20 minutes, or until a toothpick inserted into the center comes out clean.
7. Let the muffins cool before serving.

Nutritional Facts (Per Serving): Calories: 180 kcal | Protein: 6g | Fat: 15g | Carbohydrates: 7g | Fiber: 3g | Sugar: 2g | Sodium: 150mg

Glycemic Index: Low (approximately 25)

Coconut Flour Brownies

Prep Time: 10 minutes | Cook Time: 20 minutes | Serves: 2

Ingredients:

- 1/4 cup coconut flour
- 1/4 cup cocoa powder (unsweetened)
- 1/4 tsp baking powder
- 1/4 tsp salt
- 1/4 cup coconut oil, melted
- 2 eggs
- 1/4 cup sugar-free sweetener (e.g., stevia, erythritol)
- 1 tsp vanilla extract
- 1/4 cup dark chocolate chips (sugar-free, optional)

Instructions:

1. Preheat the oven to 180°C (350°F). Line a small baking dish with parchment paper.
2. In a bowl, mix coconut flour, cocoa powder, baking powder, and salt.
3. In another bowl, whisk together melted coconut oil, eggs, sweetener, and vanilla extract.
4. Combine the wet and dry ingredients, then fold in dark chocolate chips if using.
5. Pour the batter into the prepared baking dish and smooth the top.
6. Bake for 18-20 minutes until the brownies are set. Let cool completely before cutting into squares.

Nutritional Facts (Per Serving): Calories: 160 kcal | Protein: 4g | Fat: 12g | Carbohydrates: 10g | Fiber: 4g | Sugar: 2g | Sodium: 100mg

Glycemic Index: Low (approximately 30)

Lemon Poppy Seed Bread

Prep Time: 10 minutes | Cook Time: 30 minutes | Serves: 2

Ingredients:

- 1 cup almond flour
- 1/4 cup coconut flour
- 1/4 cup sugar-free sweetener (e.g., stevia, erythritol)
- 1 tbsp poppy seeds
- 1/2 tsp baking soda
- 1/4 tsp salt
- 2 eggs
- 1/4 cup coconut oil, melted
- 1/4 cup unsweetened almond milk
- 1 tbsp lemon zest
- 2 tbsp lemon juice
- 1 tsp vanilla extract

Instructions:

1. Preheat oven to 180°C (350°F). Grease or line a small loaf pan.
2. Mix almond flour, coconut flour, sweetener, poppy seeds, baking soda, and salt in a bowl.
3. In another bowl, whisk eggs, coconut oil, almond milk, lemon zest, lemon juice, and vanilla.
4. Combine wet and dry ingredients, then pour into the loaf pan.
5. Bake for 25-30 minutes until a toothpick comes out clean. Cool before slicing.

Nutritional Facts (Per Serving): Calories: 180 kcal | Protein: 5g | Fat: 14g | Carbohydrates: 8g | Fiber: 3g | Sugar: 2g | Sodium: 130mg

Glycemic Index: Low (approximately 30)

Pumpkin Spice Muffins

Prep Time: 10 minutes | Cook Time: 20 minutes | Serves: 2

Ingredients:

- 1 cup almond flour
- 1/4 cup coconut flour
- 1/4 cup pumpkin puree (unsweetened)
- 2 eggs
- 1/4 cup coconut oil, melted
- 1/4 cup sugar-free sweetener (e.g., stevia, erythritol)
- 1 tsp vanilla extract
- 1 tsp pumpkin spice mix
- 1/2 tsp baking soda
- 1/4 tsp salt

Instructions:

1. Preheat the oven to 180°C (350°F). Line a muffin tin with paper liners.
2. In a bowl, mix almond flour, coconut flour, pumpkin spice, baking soda, and salt.
3. In another bowl, whisk together pumpkin puree, eggs, coconut oil, sweetener, and vanilla extract.
4. Combine the wet and dry ingredients, stirring until well combined.
5. Spoon the batter into the muffin liners.
6. Bake for 18-20 minutes until a toothpick inserted into the center comes out clean. Let cool before serving.

Nutritional Facts (Per Serving): Calories: 160 kcal | Protein: 5g | Fat: 12g | Carbohydrates: 10g | Fiber: 4g | Sugar: 2g | Sodium: 150mg

Glycemic Index: Low (approximately 30)

CHAPTER 16: Fruity Desserts You'll Love

Baked Apples with Cinnamon

Prep Time: 5 minutes | Cook Time: 25 minutes | Serves: 2

Ingredients:

- 2 medium apples, cored and sliced
- 1 tbsp melted coconut oil or butter
- 1 tsp ground cinnamon
- 1/2 tsp vanilla extract (optional)
- 1 tbsp chopped nuts (optional)
- 1 tbsp sugar-free sweetener (optional)

Instructions:

1. Preheat the oven to 180°C (350°F). Grease a small baking dish.
2. Place the sliced apples in the baking dish. Drizzle with melted coconut oil or butter.
3. Sprinkle with cinnamon and vanilla extract, if using. Add sweetener and nuts if desired.
4. Bake for 20-25 minutes, until the apples are tender.
5. Serve warm.

Nutritional Facts (Per Serving): Calories: 120 kcal | Protein: 0.5g | Fat: 6g | Carbohydrates: 18g | Fiber: 4g | Sugar: 10g | Sodium: 0mg

Glycemic Index: Low (approximately 40)

Berry Crumble with Almond

Prep Time: 10 minutes | Cook Time: 20 minutes | Serves: 2

Ingredients:

- 1 cup mixed berries
- 1 tbsp sugar-free sweetener (e.g., stevia, erythritol)
- 1 tsp lemon juice
- 1/2 tsp vanilla extract
- 1/4 cup almond flour
- 2 tbsp chopped almonds
- 1 tbsp melted coconut oil or butter
- 1 tbsp unsweetened shredded coconut (optional)
- 1 tbsp sugar-free sweetener (optional)
- 1/2 tsp cinnamon

Instructions:

1. Preheat oven to 180°C (350°F). Grease a small baking dish.
2. Mix berries with sweetener, lemon juice, and vanilla. Place in baking dish.
3. Combine almond flour, almonds, coconut oil or butter, shredded coconut (if using), sweetener, and cinnamon until crumbly. Sprinkle over berries.
4. Bake for 15-20 minutes until topping is golden and berries are bubbling. Cool slightly before serving.

Nutritional Facts (Per Serving): Calories: 160 kcal | Protein: 4g | Fat: 12g | Carbohydrates: 12g | Fiber: 5g | Sugar: 6g | Sodium: 40mg

Glycemic Index: Low (approximately 30)

Grilled Peaches with Honey

Prep Time: 5 minutes | Cook Time: 5 minutes | Serves: 2

Ingredients:

- 2 ripe peaches, halved and pitted
- 1 tsp olive oil or melted butter
- 1 tbsp honey or sugar-free sweetener (optional)
- 1/2 tsp cinnamon (optional)

Instructions:

1. Preheat a grill or grill pan to medium heat.
2. Brush the cut sides of the peaches with olive oil or melted butter.
3. Place the peaches cut side down on the grill and cook for 3-5 minutes until grill marks appear, and the peaches are slightly softened.
4. Remove from the grill and drizzle with honey or sugar-free sweetener. Sprinkle with cinnamon if desired.
5. Serve warm.

Nutritional Facts (Per Serving): Calories: 160 kcal | Protein: 4g | Fat: 12g | Carbohydrates: 12g | Fiber: 5g | Sugar: 6g | Sodium: 40mg

Glycemic Index: Low (approximately 30)

Mango Sorbet

Prep Time: 10 minutes | No Cook (Freezing Time: 2-3 hours) | Serves: 2

Ingredients:

- 2 ripe mangoes, peeled and cubed
- 1/4 cup water (if needed, to adjust consistency)
- 1 tbsp lime juice
- 1-2 tbsp sugar-free sweetener (optional, based on sweetness of mangoes)

Instructions:

1. In a blender, combine mango cubes, lime juice, and sweetener (if using). Blend until smooth.
2. If the mixture is too thick, add a small amount of water to reach your desired consistency.
3. Pour the mixture into a freezer-safe container and freeze for 2-3 hours, or until firm.
4. To serve, let the sorbet sit at room temperature for a few minutes to soften slightly, then scoop into bowls.

Nutritional Facts (Per Serving): Calories: 120 kcal | Protein: 1g | Fat: 0g | Carbohydrates: 30g | Fiber: 3g | Sugar: 24g | Sodium: 0mg

Glycemic Index: Medium (approximately 55)

Grilled Pineapple with Coconut Mint Yogurt Sauce

Prep Time: 15 minutes | Cook Time: 10 minutes | Serves: 2

Ingredients:

- 1 small pineapple, peeled, cored, and cut into rings
- 1 tbsp coconut oil, melted
- 1 cup Greek yogurt (unsweetened)
- 2 tbsp coconut milk
- 1 tsp lime zest
- 1 tbsp fresh mint leaves, finely chopped
- 1 tbsp lime juice
- 1 tbsp shredded coconut (optional, for topping)
- 1-2 tsp honey or sugar-free sweetener (optional)

Instructions:

1. Grill pineapple rings brushed with coconut oil for 2-3 minutes per side.

2. In a bowl, mix the Greek yogurt, coconut milk, chopped mint, lime zest, lime juice, and sweetener (if using). Stir until smooth and well combined.

3. Arrange the grilled pineapple rings on a serving plate. Drizzle with the coconut mint yogurt sauce.

4. Sprinkle with shredded coconut for an extra layer of flavor and texture. Serve warm or chilled.

Nutritional Facts (Per Serving): Calories: 160 kcal | Protein: 6g | Fat: 7g | Carbohydrates: 20g | Fiber: 3g | Sugar: 15g | Sodium: 40mg

Glycemic Index: Medium (approximately 55)

Poached Pears with Spices

Prep Time: 10 minutes | Cook Time: 20 minutes | Serves: 2

Ingredients:

- 2 ripe but firm pears, peeled and cored
- 2 cups water
- 1 cinnamon stick
- 2 whole cloves
- 1 star anise (optional)
- 1 tsp vanilla extract
- 1 tbsp lemon juice
- 1-2 tsp sugar-free sweetener (optional)

Instructions:

1. In a medium saucepan, combine water, cinnamon stick, cloves, star anise, vanilla extract, lemon juice, and sweetener (if using). Bring to a simmer over medium heat.

2. Add the pears to the simmering liquid. Cover and poach for 15-20 minutes, turning occasionally, until the pears are tender.

3. Remove the pears from the liquid and let them cool slightly before serving. You can reduce the poaching liquid to a syrup by simmering it further, then drizzle it over the pears.

Nutritional Facts (Per Serving): Calories: 80 kcal | Protein: 0g | Fat: 0g | Carbohydrates: 21g | Fiber: 4g | Sugar: 14g | Sodium: 5mg

Glycemic Index: Low (approximately 40)

Raspberry Gelato

Prep Time: 10 minutes | No Cook (Freezing Time: 2-3 hours) | Serves: 2

Ingredients:

- 1 cup fresh or frozen raspberries
- 1/2 cup Greek yogurt (unsweetened
- 1/4 cup coconut milk (unsweetened)
- 1-2 tbsp sugar-free sweetener (e.g., stevia, erythritol)
- 1 tsp vanilla extract
- 1 tsp lemon juice

Instructions:

1. In a blender, combine raspberries, Greek yogurt, coconut milk, sweetener, vanilla extract, and lemon juice. Blend until smooth.
2. Pour the mixture into a freezer-safe container and freeze for 2-3 hours, stirring every 30 minutes to break up ice crystals.
3. Once the gelato reaches a creamy consistency, scoop and serve.

Nutritional Facts (Per Serving): Calories: 90 kcal | Protein: 3g | Fat: 3g | Carbohydrates: 14g | Fiber: 5g | Sugar: 6g | Sodium: 10mg

Glycemic Index: Low (approximately 25)

Strawberry Rhubarb Compote

Prep Time: 5 minutes | Cook Time: 15 minutes | Serves: 2

Ingredients:

- 1 cup strawberries, hulled and sliced
- 1/2 cup rhubarb, chopped
- 1/2 tsp vanilla extract
- 1-2 tbsp sugar-free sweetener (e.g., stevia, erythritol)
- 1/4 tsp ground cinnamon (optional)
- 1 tbsp water

Instructions:

1. In a saucepan, combine strawberries, rhubarb, sweetener, vanilla extract, cinnamon (if using), and water.
2. Cook over medium heat, stirring occasionally, until the fruit is soft, and the mixture has thickened, about 10-15 minutes.
3. Remove from heat and let cool slightly before serving. The compote can be served warm or chilled.

Nutritional Facts (Per Serving): Calories: 50 kcal | Protein: 1g | Fat: 0g | Carbohydrates: 12g | Fiber: 3g | Sugar: 5g | Sodium: 0mg

Glycemic Index: Low (approximately 25)

CHAPTER 17:
Your 30-Day Meal Plan

1 Week			
Day	**Breakfast**	**Lunch**	**Snack**	**Dinner**
1	Spinach and Feta Omelette (p.15, 220 kcal)	Mediterranean Quinoa Salad (p.27, 280 kcal)	Apple Cinnamon Smoothie (p.23, 200 kcal)	Stuffed Bell Peppers with Quinoa (p.43, 280 kcal)
2	Overnight Oats with Chia Seeds (p.19, 250 kcal)	Grilled Chicken and Avocado Wrap (p.31, 350 kcal)	Roasted Chickpeas with Spices (p.55, 180 kcal)	Eggplant Parmesan (p.43, 350 kcal)
3	Scrambled Eggs with Vegetables (p.15, 200 kcal)	Lentil and Vegetable Soup (p.35, 250 kcal)	Frozen Yogurt Bark with Berries (p.60, 120 kcal)	Shrimp and Avocado Salad (p.47, 300 kcal)
4	Cottage Cheese with Fresh Fruit (p.19, 280 kcal)	Grilled Chicken Breasts (p.39, 300 kcal)	Sugar-Free Banana Bread (p.63, 180 kcal)	Greek Salad with Feta and Olives (p.28, 250 kcal)
5	Almond Milk Berry Smoothie (p.23, 180 kcal)	Cucumber and Avocado Salad with Lemon Dressing (p.27, 220 kcal)	Baked Apples with Cinnamon (p.67, 120 kcal)	Turkey Burgers with Portobello Mushroom Buns (p.39, 350 kcal)
6	Warm Quinoa Porridge with Berries (p.16, 300 kcal)	Chicken and Kale Stew (p.35, 280 kcal)	Baked Zucchini Chips (p.55, 100 kcal)	Grilled Tofu with Vegetables (p.44, 240 kcal)
7	Avocado Toast with Cucumber Slices (p.20, 250 kcal)	Turkey and Spinach Whole Grain Sandwich (p.31, 300 kcal)	Chocolate-Covered Almond and Berry Truffles (p.60, 180 kcal)	Baked Tilapia with Lemon (p.47, 220 kcal)
2 Week			
Day	**Breakfast**	**Lunch**	**Snack**	**Dinner**
8	Baked Avocado with Egg (p.16, 280 kcal)	Roasted Beet and Goat Cheese Salad (p.29, 280 kcal)	Banana Oat Cookies (p.62, 160 kcal)	Beef Stir-Fry with Broccoli (p.40, 300 kcal)
9	Nutty Muesli with Berries (p.20, 300 kcal)	Tomato Basil Soup (p.36, 180 kcal)	Almond and Seed Crackers (p.56, 200 kcal)	Chickpea and Spinach Curry (p.44, 280 kcal)

Day	Breakfast	Lunch	Snack	Dinner
10	Peanut Butter and Banana Smoothie (p.24, 300 kcal)	Tuna Salad Lettuce Wraps (p.30, 220 kcal)	Grilled Pineapple with Coconut Mint Yogurt Sauce (p.69, 160 kcal)	Grilled Scallops with Asparagus (p.48, 250 kcal)
11	Tofu Breakfast Burrito (p.17, 320 kcal)	Kale and Apple Salad with Walnuts (p.27, 220 kcal)	Greek Yogurt Popsicles with Berries (p.61, 100 kcal)	Chicken Caesar Salad (p.30, 320 kcal)
12	Cold Quinoa Salad with Cucumber and Feta (p.21, 280 kcal)	Smoked Salmon and Cream Cheese Sandwich (p.33, 300 kcal)	Carrot Cake with Cream Cheese Frosting (p.64, 250 kcal)	Hummus and Veggie Pita Wrap (p.32, 300 kcal)
13	Buckwheat Pancakes (p.17, 300 kcal)	Butternut Squash Soup (p.38, 180kcal)	Tropical Green Smoothie (p.24, 220 kcal)	Mushroom and Lentil Loaf (p.45, 320 kcal)
14	Smoked Salmon Wraps (p.21, 280 kcal)	Turkey Meatballs with Tomato Sauce (p.42, 320 kcal)	Grilled Peaches with Honey (p.68, 160 kcal)	Tuna Steak with Sesame Crust (p.48, 300 kcal)

3 Week

Day	Breakfast	Lunch	Snack	Dinner
15	Pumpkin Spice Smoothie (p.26, 180 kcal)	Tuna Salad with Avocado (p.30, 280 kcal)	Spicy Pumpkin Seeds (p.57, 180 kcal)	Grilled Lamb Chops with Mint Yogurt Sauce (p.42, 450 kcal)
16	Poached Eggs on Whole Grain Toast (p.18, 250 kcal)	Roast Beef and Arugula Sandwich (p.34, 320 kcal)	Oatmeal Cookies with Dark Chocolate (p.64, 180 kcal)	Cauliflower Steaks with Garlic Sauce (p.45, 180 kcal)
17	Deviled Eggs with Avocado (p.56, 200 kcal)	Zucchini and Leek Soup (p.37, 150 kcal)	Cinnamon-Spiced Nuts (p.61, 220 kcal)	Lobster Tails with Garlic Butter (p.49, 340 kcal)
18	Oatmeal with Berries and Nuts (p.18, 300 kcal)	Baked Chicken with Rosemary and Garlic (p.41, 320 kcal)	Mango Sorbet (p.68, 120 kcal)	Roasted Beet and Goat Cheese Salad (p.29, 280 kcal)
19	Greek Yogurt Parfait with Nuts (p.22, 300 kcal)	BLT Wrap with Turkey Bacon (p.34, 280 kcal)	Avocado and Spinach Smoothie (p.25, 250 kcal)	Grilled Chicken Breasts (p.39, 300 kcal)
20	Chia Seed Pudding with Coconut (p.59, 150 kcal)	Mediterranean Quinoa Salad (p.27, 280 kcal)	Low-Sugar Granola Bars (p.62, 200 kcal)	Zucchini Noodles with Pesto (p.46, 200 kcal)
21	Spinach and Feta Omelette (p.15, 220 kcal)	Moroccan Chickpea Stew (p.37, 280 kcal)	Almond Flour Blueberry Muffins (p.65, 180 kcal)	Salmon with Dill Yogurt Sauce (p.50, 320 kcal)

Day	Breakfast	Lunch	Snack	Dinner
		4 Week		
22	Apple Cinnamon Smoothie (p.23, 200 kcal)	Grilled Chicken and Avocado Wrap (p.31, 350 kcal)	Veggie Sticks with Hummus (p.58, 240 kcal)	Beef Stir-Fry with Broccoli (p.40, 300 kcal)
23	Overnight Oats with Chia Seeds (p.18, 250 kcal)	Cucumber and Avocado Salad with Lemon Dressing (p.27, 220 kcal)	Banana Oat Cookies (p.62, 160 kcal)	Crab Cakes with Spicy Aioli (p.49, 320 kcal)
24	Baked Avocado with Egg (p.16, 280 kcal)	Beef and Barley Soup (p.38, 350 kcal)	Coconut Flour Brownies (p.65, 160 kcal)	Turkey Meatballs with Tomato Sauce (p.40, 320 kcal)
25	Warm Quinoa Porridge with Berries (p.16, 300 kcal)	Turkey Burgers with Portobello Mushroom Buns (p.39, 350 kcal)	Raspberry Gelato (p.70, 90 kcal)	Hummus and Veggie Pita Wrap (p.32, 300 kcal)
26	Scrambled Eggs with Vegetables (p.15, 200 kcal)	Chicken Caesar Salad (p.30, 320 kcal)	Kale Chips with Parmesan (p.58, 100 kcal)	Grilled Tofu with Vegetables (p.42, 240 kcal)
27	Nutty Muesli with Berries (p.20, 300 kcal)	Chickpea and Spinach Curry (p.44, 280 kcal)	Cucumber and Mint Smoothie (p.25, 120 kcal)	Pork Tenderloin with Green Beans (p.61, 320 kcal)
28	Buckwheat Pancakes (p.17, 300 kcal)	Minestrone with White Beans (p.38, 280 kcal)	Lemon Poppy Seed Bread (p.66, 180 kcal)	Cod with Tomato and Olive Sauce (p.50, 280 kcal)
29	Smoked Salmon Wraps (p.21, 280 kcal)	Stuffed Bell Peppers with Quinoa (p.43, 280 kcal)	Pumpkin Spice Muffins (p.66, 160 kcal)	Egg Salad Lettuce Wrap (p.33, 220 kcal)
30	Greek Yogurt Parfait with Nuts (p.22, 300 kcal)	Shrimp and Avocado Salad (p.47, 300 kcal)	Green Detox Smoothie (p.26, 120 kcal)	Zucchini Noodles with Pesto (p.46, 200 kcal)

Note: We wish to remind you that the 30-Day Meal Plan provided in this book is intended as a guide and a source of inspiration. The caloric content of the dishes is approximate and may vary depending on the portion sizes and specific ingredients used. This plan offers a diverse, balanced menu that emphasizes a rich variety of proteins, healthy fats, and controlled carbohydrates.

If you find that the calories in the recipes do not completely align with your personal needs or the plan, feel free to adjust the portion sizes. Increase or decrease them to ensure that the meal plan suits your individual goals and preferences. Be creative and enjoy each dish according to your needs!

Bonus Chapter: Shopping Guide for 30-Day Diabetic Diet Meal Plan

1 WEEK SHOPPING LIST

Fruits, Vegetables			
• 6 onions	• 2 red onion	• 150 g/5 oz Kalamata olives	• 100 g/3,3 oz raspberries
• 4 large zucchini	• 3 garlic cloves	• Mixed salad greens (200 g/7 oz)	• 100 g/3,3 oz fresh fruit
• 4 large bell peppers	• 1 celery stalk	• 3 medium apple	• 1 lemon
• 1 small tomato	• 3 small carrots	• 2 ripe bananas	• 4 large Portobello mushroom caps
• 350 g/13 oz cherry tomatoes	• 1 medium eggplant	• 400 g/14 oz mixed berries	
• 200 g/7 oz diced tomatoes	• 200 g/7 oz fresh spinach		
• 1 cucumber	• 5 large avocados		

Proteins
- 200 g/7 oz firm tofu
- 6 large eggs
- 2 chicken breasts (200 g/7 oz each)
- 250 g/9 oz lean ground turkey
- 200 g/7 oz turkey breast
- 200 g/7 oz shrimp
- 2 tilapia fillets (150 g/5 oz each)

Dairy, Cheese
- 250 g/9 oz feta cheese
- 50 g/2 oz mozzarella cheese
- 250 g/9 oz halloumi cheese
- 50 g/2 oz Parmesan cheese
- 200 g/7 oz cottage cheese (low-fat)
- 500 g/18 oz Greek yogurt (unsweetened)

Grains, Legumes, Oils, Fats, Herbs, Spices, Other

• vanilla extract	• almond flour	• olive oil
• ground cinnamon	• coconut flour	• coconut oil
• baking soda	• fresh lemon juice	• 12 falafel balls
• baking powder	• tahini	• 1 can (400 g/14 oz) chickpeas
• garlic powder	• almond butter	• 1/2 cup whole wheat breadcrumbs
• cayenne pepper	• chia seeds	• 8 slices whole grain bread
• cumin	• nuts	• 2 whole grain tortillas
• Dijon mustard	• 200 g/7 oz quinoa	• 1500 ml unsweetened almond milk
• stevia	• 100 g/3,3 oz rolled oats	• 400 ml chicken broth (low-sodium)
• soy sauce (low-sodium)	• 100 g/3,3 oz dried lentils	• 400 ml vegetable broth (low-sodium)

2 WEEK SHOPPING LIST

Fruits, Vegetables			
• 5 onion	• 100 g/3,3 oz kale	• 2 bananas	• 100 g/3,3 oz fresh pineapple chunks
• 3 red bell pepper	• 100 g/3,3 oz fresh spinach leaves	• 2 ripe peaches	• 150 g/5 oz frozen mango chunks
• 2 cucumbers	• 1 broccoli	• 100 g/3,3 oz fresh berries	
• 1 tomato	• 200 g/7 oz asparagus	• fresh dill, parsley, cilantro	
• 1 carrot			

Proteins
- 3 large eggs
- 200 g/7 oz firm tofu
- 200 g/7 oz ground turkey
- 200 g/7 oz beef sirloin
- 200 g/7 oz chicken breast
- 2 tuna steaks (150 g/5 oz each)
- 200 g/7 oz scallops
- 150 g/5 oz tuna in water

Dairy, Cheese
- 150 g/5 oz cream cheese
- 50 g/2 oz Parmesan cheese
- 50 g/2 oz feta cheese
- 50 g/2 oz goat cheese
- 200 g/7 oz Greek yogurt

Grains, Legumes, Oils, Fats, Herbs, Spices, Other

• 100 g/3,3 oz buckwheat flour	• peanut butter	• vanilla extract
• 200 g/7 oz rolled oats	• almond butter	• ground coriander
• almond flour	• 700 ml unsweetened almond milk	• ground ginger
• coconut flour	• 100 ml coconut milk	• nutmeg (optional)
• 1/2 cup whole wheat breadcrumbs	• 100 ml coconut water	• baking powder
• 2 whole grain tortillas	• 200 ml vegetable broth	• 600 g/20 oz canned diced tomatoes
• 2 whole grain pita breads	• 200 g/7 oz brown lentils	• chia seeds
• 4 slices whole grain bread	• 200 g/7 oz mushrooms	• sesame seeds
• 30 g/1 oz whole grain croutons	• tomato paste	• baking soda
• sesame oil		

3 WEEK SHOPPING LIST

Fruits, Vegetables	• 400 g/14 oz fresh spinach • 5 medium zucchinis • 1 large leek • 2 small onions • 2 small carrot • 100 g/3,3 oz romaine lettuce • 12 mini bell peppers	• 50 g/2 oz fresh arugula • 10 garlic cloves • 50 g/2 oz cherry tomatoes • 50 g/2 oz cucumber • 30 g/1 oz Kalamata olives • 1 small tomato • 240 g/9 oz seedless grapes	• 300 g/10 oz Brussels sprouts • 4 large Portobello mushroom caps • fresh parsley, cilantro, rosemary, mint, dill, basil leaves	• 1 large cauliflower • 100 g/3,3 oz mixed berries • 1 banana • 3 ripe avocados • 2 ripe mangoes
Proteins	• 8 large eggs • 6 chicken breasts	• 150 g/5 oz roast beef • 600 g/20 oz beef sirloin	• 4 slices turkey bacon • 120 g/4 oz prosciutto	• 4 lamb chops (50 g/2 oz each) • 2 salmon fillets (150 g/5 oz each)
Dairy, Cheese	• 600 g/20 oz Greek yogurt (unsweetened) • 100 g/3,3 oz feta cheese		• 50 g/2 oz Parmesan cheese • 50 g/2 oz goat cheese	
Grains, Legumes, Oils, Fats, Herbs, Spices, Other	• lemon juice • lime juice • 1 can (400 g/14 oz) chickpeas • 400 g/14 oz canned diced tomatoes • 200 g/7 oz quinoa • 100 g/3,3 oz black beans • cchia seeds • shredded coconut • 1 cup raw pumpkin seeds • 2 cup mixed nuts • flaxseeds	• almond flour • unsweetened almond butter • 8 slices whole grain bread • 2 whole grain tortillas • 2 tbsp whole grain croutons • 800 ml vegetable broth (low-sodium) • 500 ml unsweetened almond milk • 200 ml unsweetened coconut milk • 40 g/1,3 oz corn kernels	• 200 g/7 oz rolled oats • balsamic vinegar • Caesar dressing (low-fat) • horseradish sauce (optional) • mayonnaise (low-fat) • cayenne pepper • baking soda • pumpkin spice blend	

4 WEEK SHOPPING LIST

Fruits, Vegetables	• 2 small carrots • 100 g/3,3 oz fresh spinach leaves • 200 g/7 oz bell pepper • 2 large cucumbers • 1 onion	• 3 medium zucchinis • 50g cherry tomatoes • 1 broccoli • 100 g/3,3 oz kale leaves • 4 large lettuce leaves • 1 large fennel bulb	• 100 g/3,3 oz romaine lettuce • fresh parsley, basil leaves • 1 banana • 3 large avocados	• 100 g/3,3 oz mixed berries • 1 medium apple • 2 lemon • 2 large eggplants • 1 cup raspberries
Proteins	• 400 g/14 oz chicken breast • 4 chicken thighs • 200 g/7 oz beef stew meat • 200 g/7 oz beef sirloin	• 200 g/7 oz ground turkey • 200 g/7 oz pork tenderloin • 400 g/14 oz shrimp • 200 g/7 oz crab meat	• 13 large eggs • 4 cod fillets (about 150 g/5 oz each) • 250 g/9 oz lean ground turkey • 4 slices smoked salmon	
Dairy, Cheese	• 1000 g/35 oz Greek yogurt • 50 g/2 oz cream cheese	• 100 g/3,3 oz Parmesan chees • 30 g/1 oz feta cheese	• 150 g/5 oz mozzarella cheese • 200 g/7 oz firm tofu	
Grains, Legumes, Oils, Fats, Herbs, Spices, Other	• lemon juice • 2 cans (400 g/14 oz) chickpeas • 1 can (400 g/14 oz) white beans • 200 g/7 oz green beans • 3 cans diced tomatoes (400 g/14 oz each) • 100 g/2 oz mixed nuts • chia seeds • poppy seeds • sesame seeds • 200 g/7 oz rolled oats	• 1/4 cup breadcrumbs • 1/4 cup pearl barley • 2 whole grain tortillas • 2 whole grain pita breads • 4 slices whole grain bread • 12000 ml almond milk • 600 ml beef broth • 1500 ml vegetable broth • 200 ml coconut milk • 250 ml coconut water • 100 g/3,3 oz buckwheat flour	• almond butter • mayonnaise (low-fat) • sriracha • 2 bay leaves • lemon zest • fresh ginger • pumpkin spice mix • baking soda • coconut flour • almond flour • soy sauce	

Essential Herbs, Spices, Seasonings, and Sauces for a Diabetic Kitchen

A well-stocked Diabetic kitchen revolves around a variety of herbs, spices, seasonings, and sauces that bring out the rich, vibrant flavors in every dish. Essential herbs like oregano, thyme, basil, and rosemary add aromatic depth, while spices such as cumin, coriander, and paprika introduce warmth and complexity. Don't forget about key seasonings like garlic, onion powder, and sea salt, which enhance the natural tastes of fresh ingredients. For sauces, olive oil, balsamic vinegar, and tahini are indispensable, providing both flavor and a healthy touch to your meals.

- Olive oil
- Balsamic vinegar
- Wine vinegar
- Balsamic glaze
- Honey
- Marble syrup
- Cinnamon sticks
- Sugar
- Dried thyme
- Dried oregano
- Ground cumin
- Ground cinnamon
- Ground ginger
- Chili powder
- Smoked paprika
- Turmeric
- Red pepper flakes
- Saffron
- Vanilla extract
- Baking powder
- Baking soda
- Lemon juice
- Lemon zest
- Garlic cloves
- Chia seeds
- Fresh cilantro
- Fresh parsley
- Fresh dill
- Fresh basil
- Fresh rosemary
- Fresh mint
- Flour

Note: These ingredients might not include in the shopping guide, as I recommend always having them on hand to effortlessly create delicious and healthy dishes.

Temperature Conversion Table

Celsius (°C)	Fahrenheit (°F)	Oven Description
100°C	212°F	Low (Boiling point of water)
120°C	250°F	Very Low
150°C	300°F	Low
160°C	325°F	Moderate-Low
180°C	350°F	Moderate
190°C	375°F	Moderate-High
200°C	400°F	High
220°C	425°F	Very High
230°C	450°F	Extremely High
240°C	475°F	Max (Broil)

Conversion Table for Various Ingredients

Measurement	Grams (g)	Milliliters (ml)	Ounces (oz)	Ingredient
1 teaspoon (tsp)	4.7 g	4.93 ml	0.17 oz	Water
1 tablespoon (tbsp)	14.3 g	14.79 ml	0.5 oz	Water
1 cup	227 g	240 ml	8 oz	Water
1 teaspoon (tsp)	5 g	-	0.18 oz	Granulated Sugar
1 tablespoon (tbsp)	15 g	-	0.53 oz	Granulated Sugar
1 cup	200 g	-	7 oz	Granulated Sugar
1 teaspoon (tsp)	3 g	-	0.11 oz	All-Purpose Flour
1 tablespoon (tbsp)	9 g	-	0.32 oz	All-Purpose Flour
1 cup	120 g	-	4.23 oz	All-Purpose Flour
1 teaspoon (tsp)	4.7 g	-	0.17 oz	Butter
1 tablespoon (tbsp)	14 g	-	0.5 oz	Butter
1 cup	227 g	-	8 oz	Butter
1 teaspoon (tsp)	4 g	-	0.14 oz	Salt
1 tablespoon (tbsp)	12 g	-	0.42 oz	Salt
1 cup	288 g	-	10.1 oz	Salt
1 teaspoon (tsp)	5 g	-	0.18 oz	Honey
1 tablespoon (tbsp)	21 g	-	0.74 oz	Honey
1 cup	336 g	-	11.85 oz	Honey
1 teaspoon (tsp)	4.5 g	4.93 ml	0.16 oz	Olive Oil
1 tablespoon (tbsp)	13.5 g	14.79 ml	0.48 oz	Olive Oil
1 cup	216 g	240 ml	7.6 oz	Olive Oil

Thank you for choosing my Diabetic Diet Cookbook!

I wish you many delightful meals filled
with good health and great taste.

If you enjoyed this journey, I invite you to go on other
adventures with my books. Discover a bright and fragrant
world of healthy dishes with delicious and healthy recipes
that will delight your taste buds:

Made in the USA
Monee, IL
03 December 2024

72126998R00044